SINS of
FATHERS

HarperInspire, an imprint of
HarperCollins Christian Publishing
1 London Bridge Street
London SE1 9GF

www.harpercollins.co.uk
www.harperinspire.co.uk

First published by HarperCollins 2021.
Copyright © Michael Emmett

Michael Emmett asserts his moral right,
to be identified as the author of this work.

A catalogue record for this book is available from the British Library

ISBN: 9780310112600 (TPB)

ISBN: 9780310112617 (ebook)

ISBN: 9780310115892 (Audio)

Typesetting by e-Digital Design

Printed and bound in the UK by CPI Group (UK) Ltd, Croydon CR0 4YY

MIX

Paper from responsible sources

FSC™ C007454

FSC™ is a non-profit international organization established to promote the responsible
management of the world's forests. Products carrying the FSC label are independently certified
to assure consumers that they come from forests that are managed to meet the social, economic
and ecological needs of present and future generations, and other controlled sources.

This book is produced from independently certified
FSC paper to ensure responsible forest management.
For more information visit: www.harpercollins.co.uk/green

SINS of FATHERS

A Spectacular Break from
a Dark Criminal Past

MICHAEL EMMETT

with Harriet Compston

INSPIRE

For my family and the hope of things to come.

FOREWORD
by Jonathan Aitken

Memoirs of a criminal's road to redemption have never been more colourful or more convincing than this mighty rushing cataract of an autobiography by Michael Emmett.

The author, who I have known for over twenty years, is by any measurement a big man – in physical stature, in former law-breaking villainy, in sensual appetites for beautiful women, in generous friendships in dark places, in warm-hearted family love, and ultimately in the intensity of his late-flowering religious faith.

Michael's life story began in the 1950s on a council estate in South London. He captures the boisterous vitality of this unsung subculture with a Pepys-like authenticity rich in detail.

But sinister shadows soon start falling in the forms of rampant criminality, violence, a turbulent relationship with his kleptomaniac father, the early death of his brother, and, far earlier, the sexual abuse of Michael by a babysitter.

Becoming possessed by what he himself calls 'a dysfunctional, dishonest evil spirit', it did not take Michael long to rise from small-time South London crime to big-time international drug-smuggling. His criminal exploits across oceans and continents are excitingly told dramas. But in the end our villain, or hero, is arrested at gunpoint in a Devon fishing port and sentenced to twelve-and-a-half years' imprisonment.

For Michael Emmett, that event should have been the end of the story. Far from it.

How Michael Emmett found Christian faith when in prison, and was transformed by it, is the stuff of which miracles are made, bearing witness to the Holy Spirit in action.

However, it was no quick-fix conversion. True to form, he rebelled, relapsed, and reverted to some of his bad old character faults. Yet his companions on his spiritual journey, mainly from Holy Trinity Brompton's Prison Alpha team, saw his potential and persevered with him. So did his daughters Aimee, Lillie and Beth; and likewise his ex-wife and rock of ages, Tracy. There were many loving and praying hands involved in this transformation.

Today the Michael Emmett I know and admire is a truly redeemed soul, a brilliant storyteller, and a remarkable bringer of the Christian good news. His book deserves to be a bestseller.

Jonathan Aitken

CONTENTS

AUTHOR'S NOTE

This is the story of my life. Not to gain favour by sugar-coating the lies: it's a book that I want to write to say I am sorry to all of my loved ones and friends who helped me along the way. I pray by God's grace that I will see the end of the problems that were caused by my cavalier attitude.

To everyone reading this book, I hope you enjoy my journey and realize that the mountains we climb take us to the valleys of peace. I pray that you read that no matter how far you fall, how many lies or deceitful actions you participate in, the Lord is always there to forgive, to show you grace, and to put your life back on track, and to bless all those you hurt.

God bless,
Michael

Some names and identifying details have been changed to protect the privacy of individuals.

PROLOGUE

A black Golf with a police light tears across Bideford Bridge through the blistering rain towards us. We try to do a U-turn but I can see men with guns. We're trapped on the quayside. Armed coppers jump out. Then the megaphone: 'Michael Emmett, don't move. Get down on your knees'.

'Drive,' I say to Alan Trotter.

I get down in the front of the vehicle, out of harm's way. Peter Bracken looks like he's got measles from the red target dots of the police weapons.

'Drive,' I say again.

'They're going to kill me.'

'Al, drive, mate. Drive.'

Al panics and tries to drive off in second gear. It's all too late. It's over.

Then Peter jumps out of the car and attempts to dive into the sea, nearly killing himself. Reinforcements come up behind and start hitting him with the pistol when he resists.

I get out of the car, screaming and shouting, 'Leave him alone.'

'Put your hands on your head,' one of the armed coppers says, pointing his pistol at me. I can see one officer in front of me, two behind. One of the geezers has a massive handgun They have brought in the big boys, I realize.

'No, I ain't doing anything,' I tell them. It's midnight, it's cold, and there is so much noise.

'Everyone shut up!' I shout.

Everything stops. There's silence, but the chaos comes back quickly.

The armed coppers come up behind me and smack me on the back. As I go over, one of them says, 'He's got a concealed weapon.'

'He's put something in his mouth,' another says.

I've got someone's number, but they're not getting it, and I swallow the piece of paper.

They knock me to my knees. The Chief Customs Officer, who has been trying to get me for eighteen months, says, 'A penny for your thoughts?'

Starting to weep, I say, 'My three children.'

'Your what?'

'My three children. Leave me alone.'

I feel like I've taken him down a peg or two; I've taken the shine off his arrest.

'He's already talking about his kids.'

'Don't you talk about my kids, mate!' I bristle.

But I can't win.

'Stand up,' says the chief. 'We've got you, Emmett. We've got you. You happy now?'

He puts the handcuffs on me and pushes me right over. Now I am his trophy.

They think I am a tough boy. They don't realize that behind the mask is a broken soul.

1. FOREFATHERS

I was born with fear. This huge fear. I inherited it from my grandfather Charlie Emmett. A mental illness on a hand-me-down train. It was like a spiteful sting of a scorpion's tail – and it scarred deeply.

All three of us – my grandfather, Dad and I – were impregnated with the same insanity; this dysfunctional, dishonest, evil spirit. It was very cowardly, very cunning, very dark – and could be violent when forced into a corner.

Charlie was a good-looking boy but he returned from the Second World War a changed man. He had been hit in the back by shrapnel and was in a coma for weeks. When Charlie got back home to Battersea, he became the rag-and-bone man and would shuffle about with two sticks, so he got nicknamed 'Sticks'. Other times, Charlie would go to the pub. He used to drink beer, get drunk, and chew glass. It was his party piece. He hated the American soldiers and would have a pepper mill in his pocket, so he could throw pepper at them.

Looking back, my dad's family was a bit like the devil in that movie by Mel Gibson, *The Passion of the Christ*. The devil was a good-looking man, but sinister. It took you a second to see his beauty but then the dysfunction came out.

Back home in a flat in Grant Road, Battersea, my grandmother Alice would wait patiently. Born into a family of civil servants who lived in a house in Wimbledon, she was very beautiful, lovely, and kind. Charlie was the opposite: very dark-spirited and extremely violent. Then Brian – my dad – and his three sisters came along, but the violence didn't stop. They suffered a lot under their father. The only good thing was that Charlie Emmet was bright. He tried to improve his children's lives with education. So Brian was geared to working hard – and his father had high hopes for him.

Then, one day, everything changed. Aged sixteen, Brian came home to find his father with another woman. Alice wasn't well and in bed upstairs. When my dad saw what he was doing with the other woman, he attacked Charlie. He grabbed some coal from the fire and threw it on the bed. No one got burnt, but it frightened the life out of my grandfather. He stopped talking to Brian, who left home. My dad moved in with his best friend, Arthur Suttie.

A few years later, Charlie committed suicide by drinking metal acetone. They found him with the lining of his stomach coming out of his mouth. It was horrendous, and it haunted the family. He left nothing to Brian – my dad. It was Arthur who gave him a suit to wear to the funeral.

Brian, who was very intelligent, continued to work hard. He studied architecture at Wandsworth Technical College and ran at the Amateur Athletics Association Championships, finishing second. However, he had inherited his father's anger and the draw of darkness lured him away.

Soon, he and Arthur Suttie became amateur boxers.

Brian's reputation grew because of his fighting. My dad was only a small guy but he could fight. No one wanted to get on the wrong side of him. When he was making a name for himself, he fell for a girl called Betty, who was beautiful inside and out. They had three kids together.

One afternoon, my dad was in the parade of shops at Falcon Road at the end of Clapham Junction Station and bumped into a girl called Jean, who lived in his block of flats. She worked as a carpet layer in one of the shops and he fell for her instantly. Jean wasn't clever but she was bright, naturally stunning to look at, and stylish. Brian pursued her and – much to the shame of his mum Alice – left his wife Betty and their three kids. He and Jean married.

Brian and Jean moved into Stockwell Gardens Estate opposite her parents, John and Mary Watkins, who lived in a big, four-bedroom council flat. Her family was a world away from my dad's. Madly Catholic, old-fashioned, and colourful, they were very traditional south-east London people – and ate that way. Breakfast on Sunday was egg and bacon, followed by a roast in the afternoon. There would be fish on Friday nights and homemade puddings, pies, liver, and bacon throughout the week. There was always singing, dancing, and wonderful food.

John worked hard selling flowers in Covent Garden Market. He came from a deeply respectable family of handsome men, who were very honest and very smart, wearing suits and lovely white shirts. They were always perfectly clean-shaven and their hair would be styled with Brylcreem.

Mary gave all her money away to good causes. She was

a staunch Catholic; her room was filled with every saint possible, as well as water from Lourdes. Such was her faith that in the Second World War during the air raids, she wouldn't darken the house. Doing the ironing when there was bombing all around, she would tell the children, 'God's with us'.

Still, there was a little bit of criminal in Jean's family. She was one of six children, and her brother Peter was a naughty boy: a Raffles character who loved champagne and gambling, and got himself into a bit of trouble. Then there was beautiful Mary, who became a bus conductor. Johnny had schizophrenia, which devastated his mum, because it was a really tough situation to be in then. There was about 18 years' difference between Jean and her two youngest siblings: Veronica, an artist, and Tommy. They were more Aryan-looking: blonde, mousy, and blue-eyed.

Jean's family didn't like Brian at first. But she loved him, and she had the same strength and loyalty as her mother. Jean was one of those blessed people who had the capacity to love incredibly. It wasn't gooey love; it wasn't soppy love. She was just a pillar. Though she wasn't a noisy woman, you could always hear her laughing and she loved to feed you.

By the time they married, Brian had begun to fall into crime – mainly violence. Then he started to steal safes. He and Jean had volatile arguments, but he would never be violent towards her. He was very proud of her. A woman of grace, she was Brian's way out. He couldn't live without her, and he knew it. She was his sanity and his way of enjoying the nice things in life. Their life together was sexy. They would dance well together; he would sing to her and she would sing to him. She had his back, big time. As for Brian, he thought that he had her back, but he never did. Jean didn't need anyone to protect her. She was just that lady; you couldn't hurt her if you wanted to.

Love conquers all, and their relationship was like that. But the opposite dragged him back. He had a sex addiction and a number of affairs, even though he really didn't want to do all that and it didn't make him happy.

Jean got pregnant very quickly. With only two years between Brian's last child by his first marriage and my sister Karen, born in 1956, the situation caused a lot of headaches. Karen was a really frilly baby. Jean always liked to put her in something a bit glam.

Then Jean gave birth to me, on 18 October 1958, in a women's hospital in Clapham. I had a screwed-up face and a mop of black hair. My mum said I was really ugly. She was so upset about what my dad would think; but the following morning, he walked in and saw this wonderful boy.

I think that's where the contrasts in me started: the ugly bit and the good bit.

2. THE FLATS

It was the summer of 1962. We drove through the night to Costa Brava. Dad, Mum, Karen and I were driving down in a Jaguar. Dad's partner Arthur Suttie, Arthur's wife Sheila, and their daughter Kim had come too, in their yellow Mini. The most handsome man you've ever seen, Arthur looked like Dean Martin; more playboy than criminal. He wasn't muscular but smart, with curly black hair, glasses, and lovely teeth, always puffing on a cigar. His wife Sheila was like Ma Baker in a James Cagney gangster film. She would drive around in a Mercedes, wearing a mink coat and covered in jewels. She had a big outlet in London where she used to sell cheap clothes.

On our way through France, we stopped off in the car park of a caravan site so we could rest for a few hours. It was so hot in the cars that we left all the doors open. Suddenly, we heard a noise. This load of gypsies had gone into Arthur's car, then into ours, trying to nick all our stuff. Dad and Arthur screamed and shouted. We screeched out of there. When I looked back, all I could see was the dust and the gypsies running after us. It was frightening and we were all freaked out.

Our apartments in Costa Brava were beautiful but

not very well built, stuck together like Lego. The glass between the dining room and the small balcony was very thin. When you opened the door, it used to rattle a bit. One apartment was ours, Arthur and his family had another, and a famous brain doctor was next door to us.

One morning, Dad and I were playing hide and seek in the apartment. I hid behind the chair on the balcony but didn't realize Dad could see my reflection on the glass door. He came running towards me, but he didn't know the balcony door was locked. He went straight through the glass door and fell to the floor. The glass hit Dad in the chest, knee, and right foot. He was bleeding badly. I looked at him, traumatized, crying, 'It's my dad! My dad!'

Arthur rushed onto the balcony and wrapped Dad in a blanket, then put him in his Mini. Having no insurance, we were pointed to a nunnery. They stitched up my dad with black string; he was swearing and trying to get out of there. When Arthur came back, Mum, Karen, and I were waiting. He said, 'Don't look at the car. Don't look at the car.' But I did. It was covered in Dad's blood.

Mum went to Arthur, 'He's dead, isn't he?'

Arthur replied, 'Jean, if he's dead, he's definitely not going to heaven for what he's just called them nuns. That's the truth.'

The nuns wouldn't let my dad go since he wasn't fit to move. So he escaped with the help of Arthur, Sheila, and my mum. They put Dad in a wheelchair and brought him back to the apartment, where the brain doctor looked at him.

'It's not right,' he said. 'You need to get him to a better place.'

Dad was a tough old boy, so we strapped him into the

seat of our car and drove home to England through the night. I could see Dad's leg and foot pulsating. When we got back to Stockwell, Arthur rushed him to hospital, where the doctors split him open. The nuns had left some glass inside. He wasn't far away from having serious gangrene and needing an amputation.

I remember coming home from hospital with my mum on the No. 2 bus, trundling along the South Lambeth Road. The smog hung heavy over London. I sat with my legs swinging from the worn checked seat as Aunty Mary printed off our tickets. My mum's sister, Aunty Mary, was stunning and known as the most beautiful bus conductor in town. Mum sat tall in a mink coat with her bouffant auburn hair and false eyelashes. More stylish than the average south Londoner, she was always very smart, in bright colours with nice jewellery.

Mum and I looked like two Italians wherever we went. I was a good-looking kid: short black hair, big brown eyes, and always with a tan. She was proud of how handsome I was.

I looked up at Mum. 'Mum, you've got glue on your eye.' She wasn't great at putting her eyelashes on. Still, she didn't need them; Mum was a natural beauty.

We went the four stops to Stockwell Station. Our flat was just down the road in Pakington House in Stockwell Gardens Estate.

We had been in the flats ever since I was born. After the war, with so many buildings damaged during the Blitz, council flats had become the thing: long lines of identical houses. I loved it, racing along the corridors, my footsteps echoing in the concrete stairwell. There were no back fences. It was a community, a family community, mainly traditional British: Lee Martin, the Sullivans, the Whitmores, the Watkinses, the Slaneys, the Orams, and then us, the Emmetts. There were around twenty solid kids, from my age to about nine years old. There was a lot of love and laughter in them flats; real salt of the earth. They were incredible people with nothing, struggling along. We Emmetts had a little bit, though, because Dad was naughty.

That day, the flats were very empty. Usually women in their aprons would be chatting in the doorways, but I could see the Tally Man, the money-lender, who came weekly to collect any outstanding debts. He had a trilby hat.

'Here comes the Tally Man,' the warning would come.

'Say I'm not in,' the women would say.

Doors would close. It was exciting.

I could hear the arguments. 'I'll give you a pound a week,' Mrs Slaney said. The Tally Man grunted and agreed to 'give it a whirl'.

Dad didn't have a Tally Man, and we were one of the few lucky houses that he didn't visit.

We had one of the bigger flats on the ground floor. It was covered in flock wallpaper which felt like velvet. The bathroom, with a light blue toilet, was a bit small, but Karen and I had our own bedrooms. Our neighbours were in and out of the house the whole time. Food was always being cooked in the kitchen, where a rack for drying clothes, made of wood and rope, would dangle just above the cooker. Mum's food was very tasty. She would make corned-beef hash with egg on top, spaghetti bolognese, or lamb's liver and bacon with gravy and cabbage. Her steak-and-kidney puddings, made old-style, were to die for. Cheese on toast with grilled tomatoes was my favourite.

On Saturdays, we would go to the pasty shop or the old Chinese restaurant. Every two weeks, we would have pie and mash with lovely jellied eels and parsley liquor – that's parsley sauce they made using the water kept from the jellied eels. The best pies were made of suet and shortcrust with lamb and gravy. Harrington's on Wandsworth Road had queues that you wouldn't believe. Harrington's also had a speaking parrot which used to swear. All the kids loved it. My friends from school would be there, along with their mums in rollers and hairnets. I would talk with my mates, but Mum would always tell me to hurry up.

Every 30 seconds or so, there was an order. 'Double pie mash!' The kitchen was by the counter so they would never write the order out. Instead, they would shout, 'Four double pies, mash, licker, more pies, more mash.' The food used to come quickly on trays like the ones in prison, but it was tasty. The tables had an old-fashioned tiled Edwardian marble top and, if you ate in, you were allowed about 10 or 15 minutes to be in and out. I always had chilli vinegar and lots of salt and pepper on my pie and mash.

Dad would often have friends to stay. They were wanted by the police so Mum would take a Tupperware and bring some pie and mash back for tea. Sometimes I would be woken up by police raiding the flat. My sister Karen and I would stand in our pyjamas in the living room while they went through all the rooms.

The living room was my favourite place. Dad had a free-standing bronze bar with a black rim which he had bought from his drinking club in Balham. It was ornate, engraved with dragons. There were two bottles on the wall, set up with optics for dispensing measures: a Cinzano and Jade Liqueur. A print of *The Chinese Girl* by Vladimir Tretchikoff hung above it. Dad would sit in the room and say, 'Wow, that's our bar.'

When I woke up in the morning, I would smell the cold ashtray and sip my mum's leftover gin and tonic. I loved that feeling. I knew my mum's glass by her bright red lipstick.

Dad never wore a shirt inside the flat, just his boxer shorts or dressing gown. He would sit me and Karen on his knee and sing us songs.

My dad tried to be the opposite of his own father. He tried to be a good dad.

Every Saturday, I had my hair cut with Dad at Alberto's, near the bus station in Camberwell Green. Dad would park wherever he wanted to. His trick was to prop up the car bonnet, turn the park light on, and take the radiator cap off, then leave the car there. If anyone came along, he'd tell them, 'No, we've broken down.' We did it all the time.

I loved Alberto's: the smell of cheap aftershave, lots of towels hanging around, the sound of cheeks being slapped after shaving. Alberto was very Italian, near-bald, with neat black hair that looked like it had been painted on. He used to rest a board across the arms of one of the barber chairs, and I would sit there with a white apron on, looking like an angel. I had a crew cut so there was nothing to cut – he would just trim the edges, going carefully around my ears. Dad would sit there having his beard trimmed and his nails done pristine. He was spotlessly clean. So was his car; you could eat off the floor.

Dad had this thing about his weight. He was only little, but about 15 stone with a bulbous chest. Then he lost weight and became muscular. He was a smart boy: little suede jackets, colourful trousers, and brogues. He looked like a gangster, a bit like Desperate Dan from *The Beano*: a big hard face, a look of authority. Dad was a very violent man; not to us, but people were frightened of him. He had a reputation. 'Brian Emmett – be careful,' they'd say.

One Sunday afternoon, I was with Dad, Mum, and Karen. Sunday was always a family day for us. Dad used to take us to lovely restaurants, a lot of Jewish restaurants. We were on our way back from Bloom's, a very famous Jewish restaurant in Aldgate. The waiters used to be very smart, with nice white shirts and overalls. There were wooden floors, lots of reflective glass, and beams. It was very busy and very noisy, with a real sense of Mafia. My dad loved Bloom's, because he liked the traditional Jewish way. He always enjoyed things that were the opposite to how he grew up, such as nice food, stylish clothes, and being out of London.

We'd had a good lunch at Bloom's: a chicken and vegetable soup with noodles (*lokshen*) and dumplings (made from *matzo*, unleavened flatbread), followed by saddle of lamb, *latkes* (chopped potato and onion), and chopped herring. My mum and dad had the salt beef with the new greens and all that.

On our way back, we were at the Vauxhall one-way

system. Suddenly this guy started shouting at us; something to do with Dad's driving.

My dad went absolutely mad. He used to bite his tongue when he was angry; I did the same. Dad chased the guy in the car, screeching round the corners, flinging us from side to side.

'Brian, stop! Brian, stop!' Mum yelled.

After about 10 minutes, Dad came to his senses. I remember the relief.

'Get out of the car. I'm going to follow him,' Dad said to Mum. So Mum and Karen got out.

'I'm leaving Michael in here,' my mum said in the hope of stopping him. But Dad flew off with me in the car. Mum screamed.

By now, Dad was deep into crime. He had businesses everywhere, including Mac Cars, a cab firm in Clapham Old Town. Then three shops down, Dad and his partner Arthur Suttie had one of the first betting shops in London. Betting was illegal. They used to gamble on the streets, but Dad opened this office. A couple of the Great Train Robbers used to stop by, and apparently one of the cars used during the robbery was hidden back there. Although they were criminals, I really liked the Great Train Robbers. To me, they were genuinely nice people: kind, family-orientated, and non-violent. Just naughty boys.

Then Dad was arrested for armed robbery. He was bang in trouble, a lot of trouble. Dad had done small prison sentences, but up to this point he had been one of those unique criminals who almost never got sentenced. He had been on trial for some naughty things, but got

'Not Guilties' on one, two, three major cases: major cases for which he could have easily got double figures inside.

Now Dad was a Cat-A prisoner (the maximum-security category) and held on remand at Brixton Prison. My mum didn't want me to visit him, but I was desperate to go.

'Mum, Mum, I want my dad,' I said. 'I want my dad.'

So Mum borrowed Aunty Moya's car and we drove to Brixton. Dad was there in the visiting room behind this glass partition with wire mesh. I couldn't touch his hand, kiss him, or touch his face. I really wanted to, and started to cry and scream.

'What's Dad doing in here?'

I was traumatized. He was my hero.

The prison officer tried to grab hold of me. My dad snapped, saying, 'Let him go.' But Mum hissed, 'Brian!' and he came to his senses.

On the way home, our car broke down around Bon Marché, the department store in Brixton, but a guy got it started and we eventually got back.

I felt sad and was very quiet for a few days. I didn't talk to anybody except Trixie, my beautiful German Shepherd dog, given to me for my fifth birthday. We weren't allowed to keep her in the flats but we did; I was always breaking the rules. 'Look, the dog's got to go,' Dad would say. But I had fallen in love with my dog, so we kept her.

Dad continued to protest his innocence. He put an advert in the *Evening News* looking for the cockney cab driver who had driven him home on Derby Day, the day of the robbery. This would give him an alibi. The cockney cab driver answered the advert.

During the cross-examination at the Old Bailey, the prosecutor asked him, 'How do you remember this man?'

He said, 'Well, it was a great fare from Epsom Downs to Stockwell. He was violently sick in the back of my car. It was very late. I remember the name Jean. The man said, "Go and get Jean," so I knocked on this door, and this wonderful woman came out, cleaned up my cab with bleach, and made me an egg sandwich and a cup of tea, and put this man indoors.'

One day, when about six months had passed after Dad had been arrested, Mum said to me, 'Go and turn the bath off.' I walked into the bathroom and Dad was right there, sitting in the bath. The cab driver's evidence had got him a 'Not Guilty'.

'Hello, son.'

Dad was back. I was so excited, I was over the moon. I was his boy.

3. BREAKING BOUNDARIES

I flew around the flats on my green-and-white three-wheeler bike, which Dad had given me. I was five and always had the best toys in the flats. I stored them in a big box. All of my friends used to put their toys in there as well, but I was always in charge because of my big bike.

It was a sunny day. I could see Dad out of the corner of my eye, in the garden training: squatting up and down, the sweat dripping from his brow and glistening on his chest. He never used dumbbells; he would get bricks and sandbags out instead. My dad was super-fit and loved to box.

I came to a halt on my bike. The big R. White van had arrived; this massive lorry with a low side, which pulled up and down. It used to deliver lemonades, Tizers, Coca-Colas – every bottle of drink that you could imagine. Mum brought our empties out.

All the kids would be standing there gathered around the lorry, going, 'Mum, get us this, get us that.'

I loved making cream soda – ice cream in Tizer. I remember thinking, *Wow!* It was such a treat.

Mum and I returned to the flat. She and Dad were going out to dinner. I watched Mum getting ready. With an eye for colour and style, she coordinated her clothes really well, always finishing with a silk scarf in the summer and cashmere scarf in the winter. Mum had organized a babysitter called Sarah for me. She was sixteen years old, blonde, and very grown-up looking.

After Sarah had given me bacon and eggs, I went to my room and started getting changed for bed. But she followed, sneaking in behind me. She then pushed me back onto the bed and tied me up in a sheet before touching me sexually. It was like a frightening funfair ride, but Sarah behaved as if it was normal.

Where's my mum? Where's my mum? I was screaming inside.

I didn't tell anyone; I just knew not to. But it took me to a very dark place in my head. I learnt to cover my feelings up, but it was like the pea in a mattress in the fairy story about the princess: the more I ignored the trauma, the worse it got.

I raged. There was loads of rage in me at six. Attaching myself to my mum's apron, I would hide behind her leg, never wanting to let Mum go. If I couldn't see her, I'd be going, 'Where are you? Where are you?'

But as much as there was the beast, there was beauty.

Dad and Mum were really good with kids and there were always children in the house. Dad gave me the book *Tarzan*, which was as long as my legs. I carried it around the whole time. Inside, there was a jungle scene with Tarzan and his wife Jane, and their son Jack. Dad told me that he was Jack, and he would do a perfect jungle call. But he'd say, 'Never ask me to do the Tarzan call in front of anyone, because no one must know I'm Jack.'

'Okay, Dad. Do it in the car,' I whispered.

My parents would often take us to this big playground in Clapham with lots of swings, slides, and seesaws. I remember walking up the slides, and coming down facing backwards on my bum. My mum was traumatized, my dad furious.

'You wait until I get him,' he said. I ran.

I was always running away from my dad and, as much as I was naughty, I started to develop subconscious ways of coping with my feelings. The mask was always there. It wasn't madness; I just felt uneasy. The continuing sexual abuse from the babysitter triggered it big time. I felt different from other kids: a mixture of opposites; fearless yet fearful.

In September, I was packed off to Stockwell Primary School. It was an old-fashioned black-and-white concrete Victorian school with shiny floors. There was virtually no colour there, but it wasn't intimidating. The classrooms had little desks, painted either white or blue, with dusty windows through which you could see the climbing bars outside.

Most of the children in the flats went to the same school, so we used to meet under this big arch then walk together. Bonnie, a disabled child with a big head and dark hair, who lived upstairs, would see us off, singing songs over the balcony as we left. On the way to school, we used to pass this disturbed woman dressed in black, with dirty grey hair. Her husband and son had both been killed in the war, but she would sit outside her house waiting for them to come home. Everyone was frightened of her, but I wasn't. I found her intriguing.

Next door to the woman's house was Mary's Dairy, where we used to stop most mornings. It was a very traditional shop, filled with the smell of freshly baked bread. There were five of us: me; Frank, who had goofy teeth and a snotty nose; his brother Stephen; Karen; and Karen's best friend, Libby. Mum and Frank and Stephen's mother Violet used to take it in turns dropping us off. When my mum took us, she would buy a red cardboard holder containing five doughnuts. Mum would give us each one. She used to get told off by the teachers because there was sugar on them, but she couldn't help herself.

In December 1963, my little brother Martin was born at home. I wasn't allowed in the house. The screams from my mum were awful. I went around to the little park behind our flat and clutched the railings, as if I was a women's libber handcuffed to one of the fences in the city.

'I want my mum,' I screamed.

My dad came out, saying, 'Someone shut him up.' But I wasn't shutting up until Mum came out.

About two hours later, I was allowed in. Martin was a big baby, swaddled in white, lying in a Moses basket, very sweet. He became the equilibrium of the family. He had a quiet, peaceful look about him. There was no noise.

It worked out that there were sides in the family: Karen and Dad; me and Mum. But so as not to upset anybody, Mum operated in a way that you couldn't tell what side she was on. When Martin came along, he evened it out. He was in both camps.

I could never remember my brother's name. I used to run around the school and say 'What's my brother's name?' then go *Fartin' Martin* in my head. Actually, the trauma of the sexual abuse was taking hold. I couldn't tie my shoelaces up. I couldn't blow my nose.

Noticing something was up with me, my mother over-compensated with her love.

'All you do is mollycoddle,' Dad would say, and the voices of the two of them would ring in my head. The conflict went on for years and caused problems between my parents. My dad got very jealous of my mum's love for me. He was a very powerful man but also very frail inside, broken from his own historic issues with his own father. On the other hand, Dad was dying to be a nice man, and my mother drew that side of him out into the open.

During the day, Dad would go to Hendon, where he and Arthur Suttie had a car dealership, a front hiding one of his criminal activities. There were a lot of Ford Zephyrs and Zodiacs, really stylish: big white steering wheels with the shiny metal rim of the horn and the little radio. I was always over there on Saturdays and Sundays, sitting in the office, watching the cars being cleaned, and breathing in my favourite smell of old polished leather.

The car front meant Dad always had cool cars. One day, Dad, Arthur, and me were driving up Battersea Rise in a Jaguar past Millets, a shop I loved, with its nice denim jackets hanging outside. As we approached Harvey's, a plush furniture shop that sold velvet chairs, Dad and Arthur saw this guy. They parked me up around the corner and jumped out of the car, then disappeared.

I heard screams. I couldn't see anything, but something was obviously going on. As I looked out of my window, I saw this guy running towards me, hurt, bleeding, blood dripping from his mouth. He fell against my window and slipped down to the pavement, leaving a smear of blood on the glass.

My little mind was putting it together. Dad rushed around the corner, then remembered that I was in the car. It made him even worse.

After the guy ran away, Dad grabbed hold of me and started cuddling me, saying, 'Son, son.'

When we got home, I ran across to my nan Mary, who lived opposite us in Stockwell with my grandfather John. My nan was short with beautiful eyes, lovely chin, and a small nose. Always immaculately dressed, she wore nice patent shoes and carried a bag. She used to walk like Charlie Chaplin.

Nan opened the door in her rollers, and I immediately felt loved. I didn't say anything about my dad and the fight because I had learnt it was best mouth shut.

Still, Nan could see that something was up. She went into the larder; a place I loved, full of freshly baked pies, stewed fruit and butter. Bringing out some fish, Nan made me a cold fish sandwich, which was my favourite. Everyone loved her fish sandwiches. The fish came from a fish-and-chip shop on the one-way system of Stockwell. It was a proper fish-and-chip shop. If the fish wasn't used that day, they would throw it away, but the fishmonger used to save my grandmother fish for the following day. That's how she liked it. The guy would cook it for her, then she would collect the cold haddock or skate.

Mum was waiting for me when I got back. It was Sunday night: bath-time, and there would be no messing around. Dad was adamant about cleanliness. Mum used to wash our hair with Vosene anti-dandruff shampoo and vinegar to make our hair shine. I loved Sunday-night baths, spending time with my mum. I felt I was in the presence of an angel. She would comb my hair and say, 'I love you.'

But life in the flats was about to come to an end. A child was raped on the estate. My dad and Arthur chased the man around the back of Stockwell Tube Station, but that rape turned it for me. After that, I was full of fear in those flats. What had happened – the rapist taking this child into a shed – took the cream off the place for me. I was always spooked after that, and I just switched off.

4. A BEAUTIFUL LIFE

Just before my seventh birthday, Dad moved us to New Malden in Surrey to give us a chance, a life away from crime. It was a sleepy, very tidy little place with leafy areas, lots of golf courses, and parks. There was no traffic and there were never any arguments on the streets.

A few weeks after we arrived, it was Bonfire Night. I loved Bonfire Night, listening to the crackle, feeling the heat on my face, and watching the sparks drift into the night sky.

Dad stood beside the bonfire quietly, with authority, while Mum walked over with a jacket potato. An Austrian lady had made it; I watched her put oil around the potato then soak it with salt and pepper before wrapping it up tightly and putting it on the fire. They came out superbly: the fire burnt and crisped up the skin, but made it go soft white inside. The lady could see that I loved the potatoes and gave me two.

'What about the fireworks?' my dad asked.

'No, go get the potatoes, Dad.'

Other times, I heard a few whispers about my dad's activities. 'What's going on here?' they'd say. But I didn't understand adult thinking and just thought everything was cool.

We had a big semi-detached house with a front garden on a lovely road in the lower part of town. Dad was a keen gardener and the garden was beautiful, with roses, lovely big trees, and unusual plants. For my birthday, I had been given a Johnny Seven gun. I liked to hide in bushes, spread-eagled, pretending to be a marksman and shooting at the tree branches. Other times I would run into the house, toy gun at the ready.

The house was lovely, with cream and magnolia flock wallpaper; then dad had a brainstorm and painted it browny orange. Our lounge had comfortable settees with clean net curtains. We always had a big fridge, colour telly, and good music.

There were lots of houses on our street, all painted in pastel colours. It was very peaceful, with hardly any cars coming down, so we used to play tennis in the road. We had a builder called Mr Hall and his wife on one side and on the other, Mrs Blagden, an elderly lady who looked like Little Miss Tiny. Reverend Sharp lived opposite us, always outside clipping his hedge. Then there were the Wearings, the Buicks, the Grahams, the Nashes, who all had nice kids. It wasn't extreme wealth, but the families were well-off, comfortable. Everyone had two cars, but there was nothing flashy or cocky about it.

Further up the road was Traps Lane which was very posh: home to golfers, actors, and comedian Jimmy Tarbuck, who was very influential up there. Arthur Suttie bought a house on the Traps Lane golf course, but my dad didn't want the Traps Lane style. Dad was funny about houses. 'Don't let them see what you've got' was his way of thinking.

Dad was always trying to cover up that he was a criminal, so he acted like a car dealer and conducted himself extremely well. But my dad's dream really was not to be involved in crime. He wanted a beautiful life. He liked art, the next-door neighbour, and animals. He was a family man.

Dad loved to do a big family day out at Strouds, a lovely swimming pool on the way to Brighton. We would get up on Sunday morning, then Mum would pack cooked chicken and salt-beef sandwiches. All the kids would be there. It was a lot of fun.

Other weekends, I would go with Dad and Arthur to watch Chelsea play, especially the night games. Dad would never buy me a ticket; instead, I would sneak under the turnstiles, usually hitting my head. When the football was on, the road across Albert Bridge from Chelsea to Battersea became a one-way to keep traffic moving. It meant you couldn't go from south to west, but Dad and Arthur would ignore it every time. People would protest, 'This is one-way', and Dad would reply, 'Yes, we're only going one way.'

I used to go home and tell my mum, until Dad said, 'If you keep telling Mummy what I am doing then you won't come with me no more.'

Sometimes, Dad and Mum would go out by themselves. Whenever they were getting ready to leave, I used to slip away from the house and hide underneath the car, clutching on to the exhaust pipe.

'Where is he? We're going out', my dad would go. Mum knew where I was. She would come and look under the car.

'Mum, don't go,' I'd say.

'Get the broom,' my dad would say and prod me out, before leaving me with Aunty Veronica.

Then I'd be going, 'I want to phone my mum.'

'You can't,' Aunty Veronica would insist.

I'd throw a tantrum, screaming, 'But I want my mum. I want my mum.' And once I'd started my tantrum, I wouldn't stop.

Eventually, Aunty Veronica would phone my mum. My mum's voice would come on the phone and I'd just ask, 'Where are you, Mum?'

Other times, we would visit my grandparents back in Stockwell. When it came to leaving, I used to hide in the dustbin chute. Inside, I would scream. I remember the echo and everyone going, 'Where is he? Where is he?' The hiding went back to when I was sexually abused as a boy by my babysitter. I wanted my mum and I wanted attention.

I always had friends at school and I always had enemies. There were two brothers, Martin and Robert Miles, who came from a well-to-do family on Traps Lane. They both had blond hair and blue piercing eyes, like they came from Norway. Martin was dumpy and stocky. Robert was a good-looking boy and extremely tall, with trousers too short against his shoes. He was a great athlete who went on to be a top policeman. Robert used to say to me, 'Michael, the word isn't *ain't*, it's *isn't*.' When Martin tried it on with me at school, I hit him on the chin. 'Don't talk to me like that,' I warned. He went and got Robert, who I was afraid of as he was a big kid. Robert gave me a clip around the earlobe and I never forgot it.

Dad sent us to good schools. He thought educating us was a good thing to do. He was so happy that my sister was bright because he believed in that way of living. His intentions for his children were brilliant. It wasn't his pride or his ego. It was just, 'I want these kids to achieve.'

He wanted us to look good too, and would take us shopping in this one-off trendy children's boutique over on Richmond Bridge. Dad would dress me in lovely fitted lapel jackets and a double-breasted sailor's jacket. I used to have pleats in my trousers, very colourful shirts, cool little shoes, and a hat. People used to go, 'Aren't they smart, those children?'. I remember a nice brown pair of brogues he bought me, but I preferred my winkle-pickers.

The family dinner table was the family heartbeat. Dad was strict at the dinner table and didn't like people making a noise during meals. He ate very elegantly, with his beautiful teeth. When we'd finished dinner, we had to ask to leave the table; it was a must. My sister and brother adhered to it, but I never did.

After dinner, Dad would often go into his garage in the garden. It was a two-car garage which had a tiny room at the back. One night, when I was 9, I followed him and watched as he went up to his wooden workbench and put on some goggles. He then melted down some metal and poured the metal into a car number plate. Even though it was obvious to me even then that he must be doing something illegal, I thought, *Wow!*

Dad could be very spiteful. He never used to eat the rind off the bacon, and he'd say to me too, 'Don't eat the rind off the bacon.' At breakfast at the weekends, he'd cut his rind off and push it to one side, every time. One day, he chewed his rind and hid the chewed bit under two pieces of rind. I used to love the rind. I hadn't quite realized that he'd chewed some of it and I put the chewed bit in my mouth. It was disgusting. I never nicked his rind again.

Our nutty terrier, Scamp, always used to circle the table at meals. Scamp's father was a Crufts winner, and Dad wanted Scamp to be one too, though there was more chance of pigs flying than that happening. For a year, he used to have a harness, but in the end, Dad got so frustrated with him that the dog became a lunatic. Scamp used to attack the washing machine, toilet, and hoover, and bite everyone in the bum.

When I was 10, I landed the job of paperboy. Every other morning, I would get up early at six o'clock to do the delivery round. All my mates used to go on their bikes, but Mum would drive me, saying, 'Shhh, don't tell your dad.' She used to put on her big dressing gown and slippers with socks on, then we would go and pick up all the papers outside the shop on Blagdon Road.

One afternoon, we were all going to Kingston Swimming Baths. I was good at front crawl but couldn't dive, so Dad came along to teach me. This was when he was going from his fat stage to his thin stage, and he had a ghastly pair of yellow trunks with a thin blue stripe. The lifeguards were arrogant, all dressed in white shirts, white trousers, white trainers. One of them shouted, 'Time to get out!' But I dived. My dad was just about to get out of the swimming pool and congratulate me. But the lifeguard, who was not having any of it, walked round and started telling me off. I was nervous and my dad swam over to back me up.

The geezer then started having a go at my dad. There

was a confrontation. Dad told me to get out, so I did and started washing my feet. I could hear screaming and shouting. People from my school were watching. The lifeguard kicked my dad in the mouth with the front of his trainer. Dad's lip split open; blood started spilling out into the pool. Dad swam to the side, jumped out, and put both lifeguards into the swimming pool. He then dried his face and came to me, saying, 'Get ready.' The lifeguards – strapping boys – were both looking. I was proud that I wasn't frightened. My sister Karen was crying, 'Daddy, Daddy.'

Alongside the violence, Dad was a kleptomaniac. If he saw something he liked, he'd steal it; he wouldn't even think about paying for it. He was a war baby and used to steal food to be able to eat, so it was ingrained in him. Dad couldn't help himself, even when he had the money to pay.

When I asked, 'Why do you do it?' he just said, 'Oh, it's the excitement.'

He'd nick a Mars bar or a penny sweet and wink at me, then put it in his pocket. I soon found myself lured to the excitement and danger of stealing.

Across the road was a greengrocer. I was 10 years old and noticed that Wednesday was half-day closing. So, at half past three, I got my little brother Martin to come with me and stand outside the fence, which he didn't like doing. I broke in through the back garden, took this great box of oranges, and threw it over the wall to my brother. We then ran through the back alleyways and into our house, where I hid the box but took out all the fruit.

My old man went, 'What are all these oranges?' Though my mum knew exactly what Martin and I had done, she kept quiet. But Dad went and asked my brother, who told on me, and I got in a lot of trouble. Dad was horrified, asking, 'Why are you doing that?'

I then tried the only big shop we had in the village, Woolworth's. I used to take my mum's shawl and put it over the cosmetics in Woolworth's and just scoop up all the make-up. No one told me what to do; I just went and did it. I would go and give the Mary Quant lipsticks and mascaras to the girls because I wanted them to like me. I felt excited but also frightened; a mixture of opposites.

The summer of 1969, we all went to Mallorca. We stayed in the Neptuno in Palma, which wasn't outrageously pompous, but was outrageously nice and very family-orientated. The food was great, with a three-course-meal turnout. I can remember the potato soup and the little lady who used to serve us.

During the day, we would go to a beautiful beach. Dad would put oil and vinegar on his body and would go black in the sun. Mum just went black naturally. We would swim, run, and go for long walks on the beach – me in these tiny trunks. It was a real family thing and really lovely.

One afternoon a storm blew up, but later that same day we went to the beach. The sand was lovely and wet, with little fish swimming around. I rushed down to the sea. The tide was far out but the waves were still high.

I remember Mum and Dad warning me, 'Be a bit careful.'

'Okay, I'll take Martin in his rubber ring,' I replied.

We were told to only go out to a certain point, where it was shallow. Because the water was only up to my waist, I didn't realize how far we'd gone out. But suddenly the waves began coming in hard. From the beach, they had looked around four or five feet tall; now they were more like eight feet. I went up over the wave with Martin in a rubber ring. When we came down the other side, my brother was gone. Then another wave came and I thought, *Oh my god!* I had to wait for that second big wave to die down before I could try and find Martin. But I couldn't see him. I looked for Mum and Dad and saw they realized Martin had disappeared and they had jumped up too.

As the wave subsided, there was German man standing beside me. He had caught Martin.

Sobbing and terrified, my brother had his arms wrapped around his legs. I was certain I was going to be told off, but I wasn't. I think the relief that Martin was safe stopped it. I remember being shunned a little bit and thinking, *What's going on?* Mum then came and got me because I was really upset. She looked very stylish, in a red-and-blue halterneck swimsuit with a belt, and her hair in a bun. Attractively built, she would hold her shoulders back and looked very classy. Martin and I were given toasted cheese-and-ham sandwiches and cocoa milk. Soon, we calmed down. The next day the sea was back to normal.

5. LEARNING THE ROPES

As I approached 12 years old, I was beginning to get into crime. My dad didn't teach me how to be a criminal but that spirit was transferred to me, and I was like a duck to water. Already I looked, acted and sounded like a naughty boy.

We spent part of the summer in Cannes with John Chandler, Tommy Brennan, and Leslie Pitts; naughty boys who were well known to the authorities. Georgie Osborne was also there, one of the biggest names in the pornographic industry. He was wealthy, lived in Weybridge, Surrey, and stayed in a beautiful five-star hotel in Juan-les-Pins, near Cannes. Dad didn't operate like that. He would take us camping: we'd get a caravan and go out water-skiing on our speedboat. My dad loved it.

One day, I was snorkelling in low water off a private beach in Juan-les-Pins when I spotted something glistening on the sea floor – something green, something sparkly. I slipped down to get it. It was a beautiful gold chain with a massive emerald stone and a St Christopher symbol in the middle. I could tell it was worth some money, so I pulled the chain out of the sand and swam up to the surface.

Coming out of the sea like the Jolly Green Giant, I walked up to my mum, who was my princess.

She was lying there as I went up behind her and started putting the chain around her neck.

'What have you got?' she asked.

'This is for you,' I replied.

'No, hold on a minute,' my dad said as he saw the size of the stone. 'Where did you get that from?'

'Nowhere.'

But Mum didn't care if it was stolen or found. We weren't about to hand it into the local police station or hotel reception. We kept it and took it home.

A few weeks after we got back, I started at Beverley Boys' School, where I met Steve Duble. We looked identical from the back and became best mates. He was half-French and a lovely boy. Steve's father was a croupier in the West End and his mum was a beautiful French woman who was bundles of fun and loved to cook. She adored all the children: Steve, and his two brothers, and a sister. Their home on Traps Lane was really classy, like a house in Tuscany.

Me and Steve used to do a sandwich round together. I'd give my mum the order: peanut butter and jam; cheese and pickle; ham and mustard. 'Thick bread, Mum,' I'd say. Mum would make the sandwiches and wrap them up neatly in a big box with nice paper. During break at 10 o'clock, all my school mates would find me and Steve. We'd sell each sandwich for 5p and keep the money in our pockets. Dad never knew.

I flunked academically, but I was good at sport, playing for Raynes Park Rovers. We used to train in Drake House in Wimbledon, with five-a-side football on Tuesdays or

Wednesdays, then matches on Sunday. I was slightly younger than most of the kids there. But Ivor Balls, our manager, put me at left back and I wasn't a natural left back, so I never had many great games. I couldn't even kick with my left foot, though with my right foot I was like Georgie Best.

On my twelfth birthday, I went along to the Putney Vale KLG factory in my Crystal Palace kit, all claret and blue. I was standing there very excited, but then I wasn't picked to play.

When my dad arrived I told him, 'I'm not playing.'

Dad went, 'What?' and marched up to Mr Balls, who said, 'Come on, Brian, he's just not picked. He's a little bit younger and they're big, strong lads.'

My dad hit him on the chin in the car park. I couldn't believe it. Mr Balls went over, flat cap on the floor. All the teams had gone out, so not many people saw it, but I did. Dad said, 'Come on, Michael. Get in the car,' and we went home.

A few weeks later, Dad rang home and spoke to me pretending to be Eddie McCreadie, the manager of Chelsea.

I said to my mum, 'It's Eddie McCreadie. They've been watching me. I've got a trial for Chelsea. He wants to talk to you.'

My mum went to the phone. I was waiting full of excitement. She went, 'Hello? Oh, hello, Brian.' So I thought that my dad was with McCreadie.

'Mum, what did they say?' I asked.

'Don't be stupid, son,' she replied. 'It was your dad.'

Devastated, I went up to my room and cried.

When my dad got home later, Mum told him, 'Brian, you shouldn't do that.'

But he just went, 'I'm only joking.'

During the weekends, we used to stay with my grandparents, who still lived in the flats in Stockwell. My nan Mary would give me a ten-bob note as pocket money.

Dad would take me and four or five of my mates fishing in the pond on Clapham Common. We had lots of fun. There was also a crummy Ben Sherman clothes shop, which I used to keep my eye on, and where I'd buy Sta-Prest trousers or Crombies, because it was the year of the Mods.

About a year later, my nan started to lose her mind. She would go out in a lovely brown camel-hair coat with one stocking on and one of her slippers in her bag. One evening, she made a plum pie and put in tinned tomatoes instead of plums. Although she eventually realized what she'd done, she still served it with custard.

My nan then got a job at Balham cinema as the ice-cream lady. First of all, we tried to stop her, but then we decided, 'Oh, just let her do it'. She called up my mum and invited me to the cinema with a couple of friends. When I turned up with my mates, my grandmother met us and said, 'Hello, love.' We all trooped into the cinema, where I sat in the middle of my friends and started watching the movie. The films then were black and white: Sid James *Carry On* comedies, or cowboy ones like *The Lone Ranger* movies with Tonto. Then, out of the corner of my eye, I saw my grandmother come up with a torch and her tray of bits and pieces. *Please don't embarrass me*, I thought.

There were a couple of little girls with me; everyone was looking. But she wanted to give me a choc ice and she shone the torch on my face.

'Nan, I'm trying to be cool,' I said. However, the torch and the choc ice were passed along the row. It must have taken a good minute but seemed like an eternity.

I was dying inside by the time she said, 'You've got that, love? Bye, love, see you afterwards.'

At night, I prayed for my family. Although my grandma Mary was a staunch Catholic, I wasn't encouraged to say my prayers. I just did. I used to say the Lord's Prayer regularly, then pray for all of my relatives. 'Look after Granny Mary, Uncle Tom, Aunty Veronica,' I'd say. But I couldn't wait to finish the prayer. I'd be flicking my toes in frustration and thinking, *Hurry up. Hurry up. Come on, remember their names.*

My sister Karen didn't come to London that often as she'd got a Saturday job at Di Biase, a hairdresser in New Malden. The owner, Paul Garrett, wore a kaftan and Elton John boots. He had worked in Harrods, and they said that if he'd focused on his job he would have been as good as Vidal Sassoon. He won many awards.

Paul was convinced that my dad was Ronnie Biggs, one of the Great Train Robbers. He didn't believe us when we said he wasn't. We were out of place there in the town, but we moulded and grew. When my mum started going to Di Biase to have her hair done, they loved her there and would welcome her with a 'Hello, love.'

Paul would cut my hair too, but when I got back home Dad would still look at my barnet – this big mop of hair –

and go, 'Is he washed?' He'd tell me, 'Come on, wake up!' meaning I should sharpen up.

So I'd go into the bathroom, where Dad would creep up and look at me through the door. I was petrified, feeling his eyes on me.

'Have you washed behind your ears?' he'd say.

I'd reply 'yes'.

'No, son,' he'd say. 'I've been watching you for 10 minutes.'

Then Mum would chime in with a 'Leave him alone'.

Karen would be all ready to go to school, in an immaculate dress with her school bag. I would be trailing behind, with ink stains down my uniform and Dad shouting at me that my school cap didn't fit.

When we left the house, I would taunt him. 'Dad?' I'd call, and when he pulled back the net curtain from the louvre window, I'd take my cap off, screw it up, and kick it at him. He used to snap and come running down the stairs. I'd hear Mum saying again, 'Leave him alone.' By the time Dad actually opened the door, the vicar was out in his garden and he couldn't do anything.

Instead of taking the normal route to school, I would leave with just seven minutes to spare and take a shortcut across the field, running through people's gardens and nicking the apples off their trees.

I was a little bit jealous of some kids at school. My jealousy came from how difficult I found life at that tender age. But the kids couldn't see how much I was hurting.

The sexual abuse I'd suffered had now stopped, but I had begun to like the sexual sensation. I was in denial and became disconnected. A lot of the girls at my sister's school used to really like me. I would try and duck the swings to impress them, but it used to catch me on the chin. I was fearless but frightened too. The girls would write *Micky Emmett* on the wall at school. My sister, who was very bright and became the head prefect, hated it.

I started to kiss girls and would let my hands roam. I first had sex when I was twelve with a girl called Teresa, who was a year older than me. She was well-endowed and I was a good-looking boy. The high of sex worked, but it was a distorted high and began to attach itself to the old sexual abuse.

There was a girl called Pamela whose dad owned the sweet shop. I would kiss her in the bike shed. I used to charge this boy David Whay, whose dad was a big policeman, twenty pence every Monday morning to watch us. One morning, David walked into the classroom with his mum, went up to my form teacher, Mrs Newbiggin, and told her what had been going on. Mrs Newbiggin asked me to come into the book room with David's mum.

My teacher said, 'So, you've been kissing Pamela for money?'

I said yes. She didn't know what do. 'Well, you can't have the money,' she said, which I found disappointing. Then she slippered me hard in front of the school.

I continued to grow up fast. I had just learnt how to smoke from staying with my cousins, who lived in a very naughty area in the Cowley flats in Brixton. It was concrete jungle. They used to think of us as posh kids because we lived in Surrey, but I was madder than them. My cousins used to wake me up at three in the morning and go, 'Come on, we're going out.' We'd get out of the bedroom window and break into their school, where all the kids used to meet and smoke Player's Number 6s.

I had started to drink too. I first got drunk under the arches of the railway bridge between Raynes Park and New Malden. We used to sneak over there and have fun. Covered in graffiti, the arches were surrounded by woodlands, with a tyre swing hanging off one of the trees. I was with a couple of mates and someone produced Party Fours: four cans' worth of beer in one big one. I'd smelt alcohol and tasted a bit, but I got paralytic this time. We made it to New Malden High Street, where I was violently sick. I remember sitting on the pavement for an hour or two, not knowing what to do, before going home.

I was now stealing from Woolworth's constantly, and was good at making money too. Mum once gave me spending money for a school trip to France. It was November 1970 and chucking it down with rain. Everyone was sick on the boat on the way back. I bought a number of miniature Eiffel Towers and sold them to my classmates because they hadn't bought presents to take home.

I can remember manipulating my friends, saying, 'I've got a present for my mum.'

'Oh, we want presents for our mum!' they said.

When I got off the school coach, the first thing I did was walk up to Mum and return her money, plus profit.

She said, 'Where have you got this from?'

'I've just been selling Eiffel Towers on the boat, Mum.'

That Christmas was one of my favourite Christmases. Dad always made it all about the kids, and home was like a fruit shop: lots of dates, fat grapes, and big tomatoes.

But best of all, that year my Dad gave me an air rifle, much to Mum's terror. It had to be pumped with air, then you'd shoot the pellets. If I hit you, you wouldn't like it.

In the meantime, my sister Karen had joined the Girl Guides, whose hut was at the end of our garden. One day, she was receiving an award from the Guide leader, Akela. I was watching from the top of our garage, hidden behind a tree and spread-eagled Johnny-Seven-style with my new air rifle. As Karen went up to get the award, I took aim and shot Akela in the back of the leg. She dropped to the floor, holding her leg and screaming.

Oh my god, I've got her! I thought, and panicked. I dropped the gun, which rattled down the garage roof.

Everyone looked up.

'It's my brother,' my sister said when she saw me, and started crying.

All the neighbours were staring. I realized that I was in a lot of trouble. The police came and the gun was taken off me.

'I want me gun back,' I said.

'Leave him alone, leave him alone,' my mum told the police.

Among the chaos, I was beginning to get to know my mum's schizophrenic brother, Uncle Johnny, who was in Banstead Mental Hospital, near our house. The hospital was vast, noisy, and barbaric – not a carer in sight. But Johnny was the nicest guy you'd ever met. He was very striking: tall, dark, and Italian-looking, with very good eyebrows. We looked very similar. He was highly intelligent and well- mannered, but really unwell, and the illness ravaged him, although he never complained once. When he was hearing voices, my uncle would keep away from everyone. He had books on Satanism everywhere and thought he heard the voice of God, who he believed was a black woman.

Mum used to gather together socks, pants, shampoo, and food for Johnny and ask me to take the bus to deliver them. So off I went. I loved spending time with him. It was a bit like Tom Cruise and Dustin Hoffman in *Rain Man*. Although Johnny was bigger than me, I felt that I was the authority and, as much as I looked up to him, he used to look up to me. It was the blind leading the blind a little bit, but we had an incredible friendship. I loved him unconditionally.

When Johnny used to stay in our house, I would ask my mum if I could sleep in the same room as him. 'Are you sure?' she would go, but I used to like sitting there and watching him smoke roll-ups into the night. There was something about Uncle Johnny that was incredibly beautiful. He was so kind, so considerate. He wore rings on every finger and used to go out and thieve: just little bits. He had a girlfriend, Helen, also a patient, who had a basin haircut and wore maroon miniskirts, crop tops, and a really tight mac which didn't fit her.

'What goes on there?' I asked Johnny.

'We go out to the cricket nets at the back of the garden,' he replied. 'She bats, I bowl.'

One day, I saw Johnny walking through the town screaming, with kids telling him where to go. I walked up to him. 'Uncle Johnny, Uncle Johnny.' I wasn't embarrassed. I took my uncle by the arm and walked him home to Mum. The following day, my girlfriend Caroline Neave at school couldn't believe it. She was amazed that I wasn't frightened.

But his mental illness rubbed off on me. I vividly remember walking back from school and getting it in my head that I had mental-health issues. I believed it for many years.

6. NARROW GATE, BROAD GATE?

By 13, I was getting increasingly disjointed. I couldn't filter the emotions caused by the sexual abuse. My low self-worth consumed me and I learnt to behave in a way which took me away from my feelings. The dual character really came out then. I became the clown, the man of many faces, then started to get affirmation because I was good at crime, fighting, and football.

I was still at Beverley Boys' School and hated it. But my headmaster, Clifford H. Fisher, liked me because I'd just been caught smoking in the toilets and owned up to it. A small, good-looking man, Mr Fisher had a little moustache, glasses, and thin mousy hair with a side parting. Every now and again, he used to wear a nice tie. You could see that he might like a checked jacket or a checked pair of trousers outside of school. A man of authority, Mr Fisher wanted the school to be a full grammar school, but the council wouldn't grant permission.

I used to get into fights at school. I had just beaten up Steve Hanchett, who was a tough kid, but I quickly got dethroned by Jelly Carter, the forward in the rugby team. He was fat and no one thought he could fight, but he bashed the life out of me. I lost face.

My dad went mad. He said, 'You go back and you hit him. If you want to, give him a bit of stick.' He meant, keep him in line. 'Smack him right across the back. Not across the head.'

Every week, we had maths with Mr Mackie, a former prisoner of war, who had helped build the bridge over the River Kwai. One day, Steve Duble had brought in some yellow bonbons and Mr Mackie turned to me.

'Emmett, are you eating lemon bonbons?'

'No, sir,' I went, my cheek bulging.

'Emmett, you're eating lemon bonbons. Go and get the cane and the book.'

So I went to Mr Fisher's office. But he rarely let a teacher cane me. He said, 'I'll sign the book; just go out rubbing your backside.' But one day my friends and I got into trouble. Mr Fisher made up for all the times we'd got away with it by caning us in front of the school.

On my school reports, which were really bad, Mum would change my marks from a D to a B+. But when it came to football, rugby, and getting your colours, I was fairly good. Mr Fisher would be on the pitch with his basset hound, like the Hush Puppie dog. 'Come on, Emmett! Stream it, Emmett!' Then, after rugby, he would give me a lift home and drop me at the end of my road with, 'See you Monday, lad.'

I remember coming home from school one afternoon to find my mother devastated. She had just heard the news that her sister had died. My Aunty Mary had fallen in love but something had gone wrong and she'd ended up on antidepressants. She got herself in such a state that she went to bed and took some tablets. Though she didn't overdose, they found her dead in the morning. It was tragic.

I had never seen my mum cry before. I was sitting in the window peeking out from behind the net windows in the front room when my parents came back from the funeral. I watched my mum stagger out of the car; she was distraught. Dad came round and helped her. Mum was hunched and went straight to her bedroom, where I could hear her sobbing. We knew not to go near her for a little while.

A few days later, to cheer Mum up, we went to Brighton for fish and chips. On these trips, I would get home from school around four o'clock and we would get in the car. Mum would bring some blankets and put them over me, Karen, and Martin. When we arrived, we would buy the cod and chips and eat it sitting on the bench beside the beach while watching the sea. They were brilliant moments.

One afternoon, with about eight of my mates, we went to a youth club in Norbiton. We were messing around with blunt pieces of metal which we'd sharpened at school. The club was attached to a Hell's Angels group, so it was bikey and loud. Suddenly the police arrived. I ran and hid in a garden shed, and I remember looking the other way thinking that they might not see me. But they found me because of my red jumper. We were arrested for violence and taken to the police station. The police let us go while they continued their investigations.

I was marked down as the ring leader and they took away all my stuff: a ten-pack of Number 6 cigarettes and a ha'penny. There was an eerie silence as I collected my things. Dad – waiting outside with my mum, Arthur Suttie, and his wife Sheila – was seriously anti-smoking. When the Number 6 cigarettes dropped out, he looked as if a dragon had appeared. But the ha'penny was stuck in the corner of the big envelope. The wait was excruciating, but finally the coin fell out.

Sheila said to Dad, 'Brian, chin him, chin him! We can't have him in the police station getting into trouble! He needs a belting.'

Arthur said, 'Leave him alone,' and Mum agreed.

But Dad said, 'Shut up, you're spoiling him.' As soon as we'd made our way out onto the High Street, I ran for it.

Dad didn't want me to get a criminal charge. So the following day he got hold of George Fenwick, Head of Kingston Police Station – a man who was later jailed for ten years for corruption. Dad, Mum, and I went to meet him at Bentalls Department Store. I didn't know that he was a copper, I just remember the tea and cake we had; and my mum, with her bouffant hair and fake eyelashes, loving me.

On returning to the police station, we were told that the charges had been dropped. The parents were over the moon. We waited in this empty room, the kids on school chairs, parents standing round the side. Then the door opened and in walked George Fenwick.

I didn't say anything. I was programmed that *mum's the word*.

He looked at me and said, 'What noise does a sheep make?'

I looked at my old man, who wouldn't even look back.

'Baaa,' I went.

'Louder,' said Fenwick.

'Baa!'

'Louder.'

I baa-ed at the top of my voice.

'Baa baa baa – that's what sheep do. None of you be sheep,' he said. 'None of you follow what the other one is doing.'

I wanted to say, *Who are you talking to?* But I knew not to.

Still, if Fenwick wanted to put us off getting further into crime, for me at least it didn't work.

Despite being naughty, I continued to do really well at sport and, in the summer of 1974, I played football in Canada. There were about three or four schools involved. We did a swap with some boys from Ontario who had come to stay with us a few weeks before. I was due to stay with lovely little Jesse, who had stayed with us in New Malden. His father owned a franchise for Mercedes Benz.

When we arrived, we sat in the school hall waiting to be picked up. But Jesse didn't turn up. No one came. I was just this marooned kid. It tapped straight away into my low self-worth. Then the teacher brought across this guy and his wife.

'Jesse's parents have split up,' the teacher told me. 'You'll have to stay with these people.'

The couple took me to their very small apartment with two young kids who had nothing to do with the football. I felt uncomfortable. The kids looked at me through the door when I was in bed and it really upset me. I woke up in the middle of the night very frightened and not liking what was going on. Though I pretended to be happy, I really missed my mum.

After a little while I went to see Jesse and his family. His dad agreed that I could go and stay there. They lived in a beautiful house on a road called Westlake Drive. It was really lovely, and I had a little kiss and cuddle with Jesse's sister.

I remember playing some great football in Canada in the stadium of the national football team. The stadium was massive and events were televised on a French TV channel. Poland played one evening against the Canadian national side, which was amazing. Poland had just knocked out England from qualifying for the World Cup. There were cheerleaders on the touchline. I remember having a fight at the after-party on the last day, over a girl, and coming home with a black eye, a proper shiner.

A few days after I got back, it was my shift at Mac Fisheries, where I was working with Steve Duble. We were the Saturday boys, but used to work on Friday nights too. It was good money but Terry, the guy in charge, didn't like me. He had big arms and a white vest, and he was very spiteful.

The worst job was bagging up all the heads and guts of the fish from this black bin. Steve and I should have alternated, but Terry always wanted me to do it. The most horrible fish were cod or conger eels, which had really sharp ribs. I'd have to put the Wellington boots on, put my hand in the bin, and get out all the ice and horrible water, then bag up the heads and guts up in big thick plastic bags.

Every afternoon, Terry used to go to the pub. This time I said to Steve, 'I know what we'll do.' We got the bones of the conger eels and stuck them in his Wellington boots.

The guy came back after a couple of pints of bitter and put his feet in the boots. He screamed. They jabbed him hard. I was crying with laughter. I said to him, 'Don't ask me to keep doing that bin.' He couldn't believe the front of this kid – me. My mate couldn't believe it either. Terry got up and clumped me.

'All right, wait there,' I said. 'I'm going to get my dad.' Dad rushed in and knocked him out.

After that, I went to work for Safeway's. I was so proud when I got my wages every week. But whenever I was on the tills, Dad would come and nick stuff. He'd get a load of food and tell me, 'Ring the bananas up, but don't ring that up.' I was absolutely traumatized. He thought it was a giggle, whereas I just sat there thinking I was going to lose my job.

Then a family feud started with Mr Adams, who lived at the end of our road and owned the hardware shop in Kingston Road, in Norbiton. In his spare time, he was a top scuba diver. He had a little moustache and his wife was Swedish and very tall. They had two kids, including Peter, who was also very tall but a year younger than me.

One day, Martin and I were in the park. Peter Adams was there playing golf. As he swung back, he hit my brother in the nose. He didn't mean to do it, but Martin's nose started bleeding and he was rushed to hospital. The following day I saw Peter at the ice-cream van. I ran up and punched him in the ear, perforating his eardrum.

A few weeks later, I was with my mate Tony Eagar, smoking at the end of our road, where there was a massive old people's home. Outside was a big oak tree where a lawnmower always used to be tied up. Tony and I shook some of the fuel out and set fire to it with our cigarettes. I didn't expect a bomb, but the leaves caught fire. Seeing the burning leaves, Mr Adams pulled up in his Volvo. Tony ran straight across the road to the big house where he lived, but Mr Adams caught me, got me by the hair, and marched me home. Mum was there, but Dad was away, busy with his bullion-and-silver smuggling operation and illegal record business in Ireland.

As Mum opened the door, I ran into the kitchen and got a butter knife. I wasn't going to do any damage; I just wanted to frighten Mr Adams. I went to the front of the house, where he went on and on to my mum.

But later my dad and Arthur Suttie got involved. They drove with me to Mr Adam's hardware shop, where Dad said to Arthur, 'Take Michael outside.' Then he went into the shop and had a fight with Mr Adams.

Dad and I were still close. I would go down to the dojo – the martial arts hall – in Raynes Park and watch Dad do karate. He was only a yellow belt but because he could fight, Dad used to take part in free-fighting competitions. He was a good amateur and knocked a few of them out. I remember being so proud of him. I went on the pads with Dad too, but never got into it and he never pushed me. He didn't want me to go into the ring.

For a while, Dad and I ran an under-13s football team together in Cromwell Road with a load of quite respectable kids, including a lot of policemen's children. We didn't have our own official pitch, so we used a field at the end of our road. Sir Bobby Robson, then manager of Fulham FC, was a friend of my dad's mate Tommy

Brennan and gave us Fulham FC kits, with green socks, black shorts, and a Fulham shirt without the badge. We transported the kids in one of my dad's old gas lorries. It had no windows and no seats, so on arrival the kids used to be full of fumes; it was funny. I was the coach and my dad was the pretend manager.

One day, we were playing at Fitzgeorge's ground in Norbiton. With a very vocal coach, they were a team of tough kids, and they were trying to do our team. Still, they weren't tougher than me and my dad. We knew how to scrape our elbows and get back up again. Our kids were suburban children, slightly privileged rather than silver-spoon. But then there were three or four others like our centre-forward − my younger cousin; a tough kid from Brixton who could fight. Also part of the team was David, John Chandler's son, a brown belt in karate. I knew he was game.

Suddenly, the coach shouted across to Dad's mate Tommy Brennan, 'Who do you think you are? Joe Bugner?' He meant the famous heavyweight boxer.

My dad was standing in a full-length leather German trench coat like a member of the Gestapo. I saw him go, 'Oh yeah,' and start making his way towards the coach. Dad was usually quiet and cunning, never noisy, but this time he shouted out. John Chandler joined in.

'Look, Dad,' I said, 'this is just a kids' game of football.'

The coach had no idea what Dad and John were capable of. He could probably have a bare-knuckle scrap, but we're talking about two very dangerous men coming towards him who could have tied him up, put him in the boot of a car, and strung him off a bridge.

I saw the referees watch Dad running across the pitch. Then he went *wallop* and hit the coach on the chin, knocking him out.

The coach didn't get up. Dad wouldn't hurt someone on the floor; he'd just walk away. But then it all went mad. All the kids started fighting. I ran on looking for someone to hit. The referee was desperately trying to send me and my dad off the pitch.

A week later, we got a letter asking my dad to appear in front of the committee in Parsons Green.

'I ain't going,' said Dad.

We got slung out of the league. We'd been first in the league and in the quarter-finals of the cup. The kids had loved it, and I was gutted. It was devastating. Huge success and huge failure – the story of my life.

When I was 15, Dad moved us to Epsom. He had bought a lovely detached house with beautiful grounds. Inside, we had nice furniture and open fireplaces with real roaring fires. Without being a grandiose mansion, it was Dad's little paradise.

Dad loved his garden. He had friends: a toad that lived in his air-raid shelter; two crows who would whistle at him and he'd whistle back; and a black pet rabbit. When our dog Scamp frightened the rabbit to death, my dad cried. He got some brandy and lit a log fire. Mum told us, 'Leave him. He's mourning the rabbit.' Mourning the rabbit? She meant it. He wrote *RIP* in his diary for years.

One of Dad's favourite places was his allotment, where he grew potatoes, asparagus, and tomatoes to die for. He'd come into the kitchen and say, 'All right, Jean? What are we having? Leeks? I'll go and get the food.' It was his moment, and he'd go into the garden with his basket.

Right then he wasn't listening to the madness inside, his ego wasn't up, and the defective character wasn't there. He was in touch with nature and would come in from the garden with his arms full of vegetables.

'See the leeks, Jean?' He wanted to show off.

Then we'd all be having dinner and he'd ask us, 'Do you like the leeks?'

'Oh, Daddy, they're the best leeks,' Karen would go.

I'd just say, 'Yeah, they're not bad'. I had to be a pain in the neck.

Arthur and Sheila Suttie moved to Epsom too. They had a wonderful house on the Downs, opposite Epsom Racecourse. Arthur had the full works, with horseboxes and a paddock. Their daughter, Kim, was a showjumper and won Hickstead a few times. She used to jump alongside Princess Anne and Harvey Smith, the showjumping champion. We started to go to the racecourse regularly. Derby Day and Ladies Day at Epsom used to have a touch of Ascot about them. It was all very old-school.

The grandstand at Epsom was a long bar. There would be crowds of people: caravans with the gypsies up on the ridge; then the members and people in the Queen's Stand with all the hats and tails. We knew people, so we used to slip in and out with bogus passes and have a field day there. Then the Great Train Robbers, who were celebrating getting out of prison, started to come. After the races had finished for the day, Arthur would hold the best parties at his house, with everyone diving into the swimming pool. It was absolutely brilliant.

As I approached 17, my crime was gathering speed. My eyes were roaming after girls. There were cigarettes in my mouth, and drink. I was becoming one of the boys. I was a strapping lad and looked like an East London bank robber, partly influenced by the skinhead era and partly by my dad, who was very trendy in beige cavalry twill trousers, oxblood shoes, and a suede jacket.

I was at school, but not at school – getting ready to leave. I remember falling out with all my friends there. I got blackballed and everyone left me alone. Even Steve, my best mate, went with the crowd. It really upset me. I never turned up for any of my O levels, so Dad got fined. I even dropped my sports, which had propelled me through school – rugby, football, swimming. I hadn't been the best, but I was above average. I'd won a few medals and had a few heroic moments. But I was a broken child, so I couldn't keep the game going.

7. REBEL

Having been protected in Epsom, I was now let loose in Battersea, where I stayed in a flat owned by my half-brother, Brian. He was doing ten years in prison for armed robbery. I continued to gravitate towards crime, with the violence, sex addiction, and illegal activities escalating. I started taking drugs, and loved it. But the sexual abuse from my childhood was playing havoc with me.

My first relationship was with an Irish girl called Trisha. I thought she was my first love. She was a beautiful soul and looked like butter wouldn't melt in her mouth, but she knew how the roses would grow. The nice man and the broken man in me became very apparent. I used to get into loud, screaming, jealous rages, but we went ahead and moved in together in a self-contained flat in Battersea.

In the meantime, my sister Karen, who was very intelligent and hard-working, had gone to study English Literature at Liverpool University. My dad was so proud. My brother Martin, a free spirit, was still at home in Epsom. He was a beautiful human being who ticked every single box.

I ticked Dad's own box, but Dad didn't like that. I had become something he didn't want me to be.

To keep me out of trouble, Mum gave me a job at her café, a takeaway for lorry drivers on a railway siding next door to Emmanuel School in Battersea. I lived around the corner with Trisha and would wake up at six in the morning to open the café. I would get all the cakes and coffee ready, do the sausages and bacon. It was the first thing that I'd ever taken responsibility for, and I learnt that I could communicate with people.

After my shift there, I worked at Dad's car and lorry pitch, New Wandsworth Commercials. Dad would steal the spare wheel and jack from each of our lorries, then clean the wheels and line them up on the wheel rails. When we were selling the vehicles, he'd ask me, 'Michael, do you have a wheel for a Bedford TK?' I would sell the stolen wheel back to the buyer and get fifteen quid. Dad also gave me a crooked MOT book with his own stamp. So instead of putting the cars through an MOT, he would pretend to go to the garage next door but simply write out the MOT, stamp it, and charge the geezer a tenner.

I started to see these infamous faces appear at work. I vividly remember meeting Eddie Richardson, of the Richardson Gang, for the first time. He'd just come out of prison after being away for ten years for torturing a man. He had black eyes, black eyebrows, and black hair, as if someone had painted him. You could see that he was a tough man. Then I met one of the big safe-crackers, John the Bosch, and Frankie Fraser, a gangster twice certified insane, who had spent a total of forty years in prison. Dad was as tough as the gangsters, but I don't think he would have enjoyed killing anybody: that wasn't his thing. Still, pound for pound, not one of them would have fought with him.

One day, I was sitting in the office and I saw the police arrive. A fleet of brand-new Mercedes had just come in from Germany and the coppers were accusing my dad of ringing the cars – changing the number plates on them. They steamed into the yard like the SAS. I had my feet up on the desk when one of the coppers walked in.

'Put your feet down,' he said.

I said, 'Who are you talking to?'

'What?' He was livid.

Dad wasn't charged but it was a heavy situation for him. Me? I was used to coppers.

Next door to the lorry pitch was a goods yard where about 200 people worked. I used to buy a whole load of eggs from a nearby farm and have an egg round. Everyone used to get their eggs off me on Friday night and I'd earn some extra cash.

With my wages, Dad used to let me buy stolen clothes like Slazenger jumpers, Schneider T-shirts, and cashmere scarfs from shoplifters, or 'hoisters', as we called them. You could order what you wanted, such as a lovely suit from Harrods, and just give the hoisters your size. If the suit was £100, you paid a third. My great aunt, Shirley Pitts, was known as the Queen of Hoisters. She was one of the best in London and once nicked a £5,000 blue Zandra Rhodes dress, which Zandra Rhodes allowed her to be buried in.

By 19, I was a rascal, fighting and taking drugs. The rebel was out. I could drive and would cause trouble by nicking petrol and smashing up my dad's cars. Dad knew, but I was a big, strong boy and beginning to be too powerful for him. He needed my mum to contain me.

Karen was now finishing her last year at university. She used to bring her friends home for the weekend. The girls would get the guitar out and play 'You're so vain' by Carly Simon and that sort of stuff. My mum would do a lovely dinner. Dad would get a fire going and tell me, 'You get out.' He wasn't embarrassed about me but liked to just sit there, listen to the singing, and savour the moment. My dad used to have a guestbook which all of Karen's university mates would sign. He loved that guestbook and would show it to his friends, saying, 'Look what Karen's friends have written'. It was his dream.

After leaving university, Karen won a prestigious award which, coincidentally, was going to be given to her by my ex-headmaster. Dad made sure I went along. My headmaster walked up to the rostrum, holding a microphone and went, 'This award is being given to Karen Emmett—'

Then he looked at my sister, who was standing on stage. 'Surely, you're not Michael Emmett's sister? How can he be your brother?'

He had taken the cream right off Karen and her achievement. My dad looked at me and said, 'You ruined it.' I found it funny, and Mum giggled.

That year, Dad threw a great New Year's Eve party. Uncle Peter was there and arrived late with Brian Wright, Britain's most successful cocaine smuggler – known as 'the Milkman', because he always delivered. Brian was very handsome and a great character, I remember him singing 'The Fields of Athenry'.

The following day, Dad was shipping a white Toyota to Ghana, which he'd sold for £890. We used to buy cars from

Belgium, which had very stringent MOTs, so a lot of the cars became saleable elsewhere because they had failed their test. They were second-hand BMWs and Mercedes, which we bought for nothing. They were all left-hookers – left-hand drives.

During the New Year's Eve party, my dad was all loving towards me. 'Come on, son, we've got to get this together,' he said. 'Will you take the car up to London?'

'Yes, of course, Dad.'

'Be careful of the brakes,' he warned me.

New Year's Day, my girlfriend Trisha and I were in the Toyota, going down the dual carriageway at Morden, beside the Unigate Dairy. The central reservation had a few gaps where you could do U-turns or turn right. Up ahead was a Unigate lorry, then directly in front of us a small yellow mini with two elderly women in it. I decided to overtake the lorry, but the elderly driver turned to go right without indicating. In a normal car, I would have had enough time to brake, but these brakes were no good. The Toyota went underneath the back of the lorry and spun around, and the bonnet and the wing mirrors flew off. As I came around, I saw that the old woman's car had been knocked across the road and hit a kerb.

'Run,' I said to Trisha.

'We can't,' she replied.

'We've got to run.'

The lorry stopped and I went over to the elderly ladies. They were okay, but the car was dented. We swapped details, although mine was a Belgian number plate. I managed to drive the Toyota about 30 yards before parking it up around the corner. As I was towed back home, I saw my dad waiting with my mum. I started laughing nervously. He snapped. I ran.

A few weeks later, Dad invited me back to work. But I lent my mate Russell a car and it caught fire.

Sitting in the office, asleep with my feet up on the desk, I woke up to find my dad in front of me. He was angry. I ran into the long building next door, which contained the spraying mechanics, and out the other end. It was snowing hard but I could hear my dad coming up behind me. I was young and fit so I jumped the fence in front of me. Dad tried to follow but skidded and hit the fence instead.

'I'll kill you when I get you!' he shouted.

I went, 'Bye, bye!' and ran off.

Dad had had enough, so then I started handling stolen antique furniture. Dishonesty was impregnated in me. There were five of us in the gang and we'd go out stealing once a day, making about £100 each time. We were like Fagin's little troops, meeting every morning at the Mona Lisa on King's Road in Chelsea. Our patch was the hallways in Eaton Square, Belgravia, or in Harley Street, where there was normally a lovely piece or two of antique furniture. Some of them were prizes – particularly the chairs.

We never broke into anyone's house. Instead, we'd ring the doorbell, pretending to be engineers from an intercom company.

'We've got a spate of burglaries in the area,' we'd say. 'Please press your bell to make sure it works.' They'd press their bell, the door would open and we were in.

Or we would try one of the private dental surgeries. The receptionist would be busy with appointments, so we would just say, 'We're here for your lovely chairs, which need restoring.'

'Oh yes, they're in there,' the receptionist would reply, pointing us in the direction of the waiting room. We were like stuffed peacocks, walking out with these expensive chairs.

We always parked the car wherever we wanted and just put the bonnet up. Our car radiator used to overheat so we had a two-litre can of water to cool the radiator down and make it steam. If we got stopped, we'd just go, 'Oh, we've got a radiator problem.'

One morning, I went into a Georgian office block in the West End to ask if we could fill up our can of water. As I went downstairs, I looked up the stairway and saw a beautiful French Boulle clock on the first floor. I saw the key was in the lock so I unlocked the door then just left the key there.

That night, Tony and I spun a coin to see who was going into the building first, and I lost. I walked in since the door remained unlocked and then returned to the car. If the building had a silent alarm, the Police would be there within moments. We waited for about half an hour but no one turned up, so we let ourselves into the basement of the building. We then spun another coin to decide who was going to remove the clock, and this time Tony lost.

After he came back down with the clock, we split two bin bags of rubbish, putting half of the rubbish in one bag along with the clock. But as we were coming up from the basement two uniformed coppers appeared at the top of the stairs. They were just talking to each other, but they were blocking the gate.

I knew that Tony would lose it. A strapping lad with sideburns, Tony was handy, knowledgeable about antiques, and willing enough, but he operated at 70 per cent. You had to operate at 110 per cent.

There was nothing we could do. I said to Tony, 'You've just got to walk out. There's no going back, mate. Just keep going.'

I opened the gate. The coppers turned around and looked at me.

'Evening, sir,' I said.

'Evening,' they replied.

As we emerged, it turned seven o'clock. We walked past the officers but suddenly the clock chimed. Tony was traumatized. Fortunately, the church clock nearby also struck seven.

I said, 'Isn't that a lovely chime?'

Tony replied, 'Oh yes, what a lovely chime.'

The coppers were looking, so we put the rubbish in the bins – clock and all. An hour later we went back. The clock was still there. We picked it up and sold it.

By now, it was summer and the debutante balls were beginning to take place, including a big one at Berkeley Square. I decided to get inside.

Princess Anne and Princess Di were both there, along with their minders, who looked like they were straight out of a James Bond movie. I jumped the railings, but you had to have a proper bib and tucker. One of my mates was a waiter there. He said, 'If anyone asks you, say you're working for the catering team for the singer, Lonnie Donegan.' I got in and started drinking champagne, but they rumbled me. I remember looking up and seeing one of the royals grin at me as I was frogmarched out.

Often I would hang out at a restaurant club called the Gasworks in Fulham, which was full of antiques. Princess Margaret and her boyfriend Roddy Llewellyn used to go there. It was run by a guy called Jack, a friend of my dad's, who thought he'd become a sporty antiques dude so he would wear cravats and all that. I was good friends with his sons, two great characters who I was very close to. The Gasworks was like Aladdin's cave, with a narrow door so no one could steal anything. It had a bell and if you didn't know where the bell was, you weren't getting in.

In the meantime, me and Trisha had broken up and I started going out with Tracy Foreman, niece of the gangster Freddie Foreman. She was a very nice girl and hot to trot. We went with my parents, my brother Martin, John Chandler and his son David, to Mojácar in southern Spain to visit my dad's mate, Gordon Goody of the Great Train Robbery.

Gordon had opened a beach bar there called the Kon-Tiki, named after the famous raft 1947 expedition to the Polynesian Islands. A bit of a celebrity in Mojácar, Gordon also owned two apartments where we stayed, and Billy Rashbrook joined us with his wife Renee. She couldn't bear the sun and never brought a bikini with her. Every day, she used to hide in the rocks by herself, take her top off and lie down in her very old-fashioned black bra. She looked like the lady from Popeye. David and Martin used to go, 'Look at her bra, look her bra!'

Gordon Goody was smoking cannabis, so I had a go. I started puffing and getting stoned with him, loving it, but hiding it from my parents. Opposite our apartment was a bar run by two gypsies – one lame, the other a young lad – who were earning money and entertaining people. Gordon had given his guitar, which he had kept in prison with him for fifteen years, to the guy in the wheelchair. People used to love watching this man play.

Also in the gypsies' bar was John Chandler, who had just come out of prison in Thailand and was a bit disturbed. There was a car dealer from Manchester too, who had a big fat belly and wore gold rings and gold watches, and was going out with one of those trophy girls, pretty and shapely. John could get very aggressive when he'd had a drink. Something happened and he naughtily touched the girl's bum. The fat Mancunian attacked John, which was a big mistake. John hit him right over the head with a bottle of Sylvester. The Mancunian was gone – on the floor. John walked out, but the young gypsy who owned the bar ran after him.

I was having a shower but I could hear the chaos and saw my dad rushing downstairs with Billy Rashbrook, Martin, and Johnny's son David. I got out of the shower, quickly dried myself, and made my way around the back to the bar.

When I arrived, my dad, John, and the young gypsy – who had a big knife sticking out of the back of his trousers – were in a semicircle. The gypsy was talking to my dad. My dad was trying to be diplomatic, but after two minutes this guy wasn't having it. I saw my dad's eyes glaze over. He was at war.

The young gypsy went for my dad with the knife. I rushed in from behind, looped my arm through the guy's arm, and sent him spinning. I hit him on the chin and told him, 'Don't stab my dad.' The gypsy fell to the floor, but the guy in the wheelchair pulled out an old Spanish gun from under his blanket. Then David, a brown belt in karate, came forward and kicked the wheelchair. The guy fell out. We picked the man up from the floor; he was fuming and went straight to Gordon Goody.

Gordon was devastated. He knew that something like this could cause trouble. The knife was taken away from the young gypsy, who told me, 'You wait!'

That night, John and I looked out of the window. The gypsies had called their mates and there were twenty lorries outside. All the guys were by the bar, sleeves rolled up and braced for a fight. They were not there for a night out.

The following day, the gypsies tried to fight me and John at the fish market. We ran and got away. They then took all the wheels and lights off Billy's car. It was insane. Gordon's reputation of being a Train Robber, and the gift of his guitar, spoke volumes, but he couldn't get us total freedom from the gypsies. It was their way.

On our way back, I remember my dad being irate because I had stolen something and nearly got caught. I thought he was angry with me for stealing, but he was angry because I'd had the devilment to do it and also nearly failed.

Back in London, I continued to do what I wanted to do. I dressed how I wanted to dress. Whenever I stayed at home, Dad locked his bedroom because he knew I liked to borrow his leather jacket. I would wear it with a pair of white leather boots which I'd just bought.

On the afternoon of 20 November 1978, I was wearing these white boots, a white pair of trendy Chelsea trousers, and a white T-shirt when Mum asked me to collect Dad from the Ranelagh Yacht Club. I arrived to find every villain in west London there. By the jukebox, I could see Johnny 'Biffo' Bindon, who'd had an affair with Princess Margaret. My dad was in the corner with two well-known London gangsters. Then there were Johnny Darke's folk, who were tough men.

Suddenly there was some dialogue between Biffo and Darke. Darke stabbed Biffo, who fell to the floor. Biffo then pulled a Bowie knife out of his boot. A Bowie knife isn't something you want to play with. Biffo apparently cut Darke across the spleen. It was naughty. Blood was spraying everywhere. Everyone ran. Darke was dying; his body went limp. His mates carried him out of the Yacht Club and propped him up against a car, but Darke died shortly afterwards. Biffo survived and was later acquitted. But what astounded me was that I wasn't frightened. Covered in blood, I'd just been devastated that my white boots were ruined. The real Michael didn't care about the violence.

8. NAUGHTY

As I turned 21, it all started to evolve. I was coming of age but still very broken. I would behave like a lunatic, the next day like a coward: completely fearless or completely fearful. Though I was Brian Emmett's son, that reputation was a mask and I was just playing a role.

I was attracted to blonde, blue-eyed girls, who were highly sexed and often high. Always having affairs, I would never finish a relationship and be on my own. I hated hurting women, yet I hurt them badly. It was part of my ego that women always loved me when I left them. I could never do reality; I could never do love. I didn't understand that *love* was an action verb.

The distortion caused by being sexually abused at such a young age was very powerful. The excitement of pleasing the babysitter, the excitement of stealing from Woolworth's, was all related. It was a dysfunctional sensation, the buzz of it all.

I loved to spend time at J. Arthurs, a nightclub on New Kings Road. Run by a guy called John French, it was meant for the stars, the Mick Jaggers and David Bowies of this world. It was really cool and chic, done up in browns and beiges, with lovely settees. There were drugs, pretty women, and a restaurant with excellent food. I was barred constantly, but Luigi, a part-owner, liked me, so he let me sneak in round the back.

John French was having an affair with Maureen Cronk, a Page-3 model who went under the name Polly Dillon. I started having a thing with Maureen as well. Well-known for being a wild child, she was the hottest chick in town, twelve years older than me, and she loved a villain. She was very addictive, very beautiful, and very crazy.

One night at J. Arthurs, Maureen took me back to John French's flat, adjacent to the nightclub, which had a jacuzzi. We then went on to her house, where the front room was full of her modelling photos. Maureen was a raging addict and we spent the next three days sniffing cocaine. I ended up living with her for nine months. I was smoking freebase cocaine (cocaine that's been refined by heating) and it was way out of my remit. Life became very volatile and my addiction grew hugely. I got really skinny and was in a terrible state.

Dad tried to rescue me on many occasions, but he couldn't cope with me. I simply sat on that mat of crime — one I didn't create. The mat was there for me already, and Dad just had to move over a little bit.

I was never sure what Mum thought. She would hide her pain. Used to my father's illegal activities, she just accepted mine. She would accept the financial benefit from me, but didn't like the violence.

One day, Dad snapped. We had just been told that my cousin had hanged himself in America. I was with

Maureen using coke in my dad's house. I shouldn't have been, but he never knew. Then an argument started between me and him. Dad looked at Maureen and said, 'You're influencing my son with all these drugs. Get out of my house.' A bottle of wine got spilt in his beautiful home.

Taking me outside, Dad pulled out a knife and stabbed it into a patch of grass outside. He looked at me and went, 'Go on, you go for it.' He was kneeling with his hands behind his back, calling me a coward and telling me, 'Go for the knife.'

Too frightened, I just said, 'You mug.'

Looking back, it was a shot in the dark. Subconsciously he knew that I was getting stronger and could see the madness within me, but also recognized that I was a very gentle yet confused boy.

My mother came out and kicked him and he fell on the ground. He stood up and said, 'Son, I'm really, really sorry', and embraced me. Then he head-butted me, breaking my nose. That was how Dad lived his life. If anyone was in his space or upsetting his wellbeing, he would challenge them with his fists. But it was at that moment that the resentments really started to cut deep.

Shortly afterwards, I met Tracy Bolton. Our families had known each other on and off for years. She was very closed down and her dark stuff caused dysfunctional behaviour, but she was really beautiful. I bumped into her in the pub one day and said, 'Do you fancy dinner one night?' I soon finished with Maureen, and Tracy ended things with her guy. We then got together.

I had just started working with Dad on a long firm – a company set up as a swindle – which I didn't know was illegal. We supplied mints to pub vending machines. The name, Flick a Mint, was inspired by a Tic Tac advert: *Why flick a mint with one flavour when you can flick a mint with two?* We bought eighty vending machines from a legitimate company and put them in pubs across London. We had a beautiful office in Motcomb Street in Belgravia, with a very posh secretary called Sabrina, who I had a little affair with. We looked good and hired proper cars; a red Escort for me. After advertising in a franchise magazine, we had these Indian guys investing in the company – ten vending machine sites for £10,000. We would put their mints in the first time round then when the machine was empty, they'd come back to us for more mints, except now they were fake mints. After six months, we folded the company. The office, cars, Sabrina – all gone. I had the master key so my dad told me to empty the money from the machines. I went round for two days, returning with bags and bags of change.

At first, Dad found it hard that I was involved in crime, but then I became an asset to him. My dad had a dual personality, going from being a really dysfunctional person to really wanting to be something good. That's the duality I inherited.

One night, my mate Tony and I stole a mirror from a hallway in Notting Hill Gate, which we sold to a guy at The Furniture Cave on King's Road, Chelsea. As I was walking down to collect my money, I saw two guys standing near the entrance and immediately knew they were coppers.

The shop owner said, 'There he is!' The coppers turned, but I ran and got away.

Still, the following morning I went round to Tony's and we decided to give ourselves up at Chelsea Police Station. We thought they just had one mirror, and we came with a cock-and-bull story. But they'd built a dossier and they put us in Brixton Prison. I remember I was wearing a lovely cashmere jacket.

Brixton was a remand prison, so there was always a feeling of hope inside, but it also had really tough prison officers. On arrival, I had to be deloused: I stripped naked and they threw the delouser over my head and elsewhere, and hosed me down. Then I dried myself, got ready, and went out onto the wing.

A number of people knew my dad there. 'You're Brian Emmet's son?' they'd say, and for a while I enjoyed the idea of being Brian's boy. But there was an expectation that came with it. As much as I used to like it, I also didn't. In the end I'd tell them, 'No, I'm Michael.'

About six months later, on 21 September 1981, we went to court and walked free with a fine of £800.

While I had been inside, my nan Mary Watkins had got more and more unwell. She had now lost her mind. Just after I went into Brixton Prison that April, the Brixton Riots had kicked off. Living about 400 yards away from Brixton Academy, with her bedroom at the front of the flats, my grandmother had heard all the sirens and everything else going on. She got out of bed, put her dressing gown and slippers on, and walked down there. An hour or two later, in the early hours of the morning, my Aunty Veronica got a knock on the door. There were two police officers standing there with my grandmother in her dressing gown. She had gone right up to the riots and started tapping the police, saying, 'What's going on?'

A few months after I was released, my nan was on the brink of dying. I was on drugs and went up there the last night. I remember being very frightened about going in to see her, but my Aunt Veronica said, 'Look, she hasn't got long to go.' In the bedroom, there was a smell of ointments, urine, and death. She wasn't unconscious but she wasn't coherent, and she looked diabolical. I thought, *I can't have it!* Walking out of the room, I cried and then left.

I rushed back over there in the morning, but Nan was dead. When I went in to see her on my own, I saw her peace restored. Bending over, I kissed her goodbye.

It was an incredible funeral, packed to the brim with hard-working people. As the night of the funeral was unwinding, I went into my grandfather's bedroom to find him and his brothers singing. They were all wearing lovely white shirts, beautiful ties, pinstripes, smart clean shoes, and trilby hats. As my grandfather John sang, his heart was breaking. He said, 'I loved my Mary very much. Much as she drove me mad, I loved her.'

By now I had left behind handling stolen goods and was getting more involved in the drugs business. What runs in the criminal mind is the adrenaline and excitement, but then it becomes about the money. You learn to be very careful when meeting someone, talking on the phone, or going anywhere. I would get a train to Clapham Junction, then walk to Clapham South to make sure I wasn't being followed.

I had been asked by my dad to pick up a substantial amount of money, which I hid under the seat of my car. I was driving down Bagleys Lane, where they were building Chelsea Harbour, and pulled around the corner to find all the coaches parked for the away supporters of the Chelsea game. You couldn't turn, go right, or go through. It was all no entry.

I could see police checking the cars ahead and doing breathalyzer checks. My thoughts turned to how suspicious the money might look; the last thing I wanted to do was lose it. There was a queue of vehicles, so I took my chance and got out of the car. Lifting the bonnet of the Peugeot, I poured water on the radiator – like we did when stealing furniture. The car steamed.

In the back of my car was about an arm's worth of plastic buckets from a flower pitch I was involved in, but there were a few flowers left. Quickly, I split up the cash among the buckets. By now, all the cars had gone. There were four coppers standing there: three policemen and one policewoman.

One of the coppers saw the steam coming from my car and said, 'He's broken down.'

Another copper, who was a mechanic, took a look and agreed the radiator was in trouble. Then they said, 'What have you got in the back, mate?'

'Oh, flowers and that.'

The policewoman had been standing there without saying a word, but I was very aware of her. Now she asked me, 'You been drinking?'

'Yes, I've had a pint of beer.' I knew I would pass the breathalyzer test.

'Okay, I won't breathalyze you,' she said.

The coppers were looking through the boot. 'Don't touch all that,' I told them. 'They're perishables, mate.' I balanced the stack of buckets between my hands. The policewoman was watching me intensely. 'I can manage,' I said.

The coppers lifted the spare wheel up, but didn't find anything, so they said, 'Go on then, mate.' Still the woman was staring at me. I put the buckets back in the boot and maintained my coolness. One of the coppers helped me start up the car; they were being all friendly.

Then the woman put her hand on my arm. 'I know you're up to no good,' she said.

'I don't know what you're talking about.'

'You'll always get caught. Maybe not tonight, but you'll be caught. I've got me eye on you.'

I just went, 'Okay.'

The other copper said, 'Oh come on, it's getting late. Come on. Paperwork.'

I drove off around the corner and had a cigarette.

Around the same time, my dad and his mate Roy Atkins were running unlicensed boxing matches in the Dog and Fox in Wimbledon. Dad and Roy then went their own ways and Dad's business partner Joe Pyle got involved. Joe didn't have the same style my dad had. Joe was a beautiful man. He dressed more like a gangster, whereas Dad was more into fashion. Dad turned the boxing competition into a dinner and dance up in Wimbledon, which was attended by most of the London flat noses – the London villains. The first night was a full house. The food was diabolical but the ambience was nice.

A few weeks later, the boxing board were coming down to give us our licence. So my dad said to the bouncers, 'Anyone who starts trouble in here, be heavy-handed with them.'

I got involved with a skirmish at the bar, arguing with this guy. One of the bouncers grabbed me; I remember my feet not touching the ground.

Joe Pyle came running over. 'It's all right,' he told them. 'He's Michael. It's Brian's son.'

Then my dad came over, and he said to the bouncers, 'Chin him.' I was shocked.

The bouncers took me out to reception. The guy who I'd had an argument with was there. Dad stood between us and started talking, but I hit the guy over my dad's shoulder.

'You'd better run,' Joe said to me.

I ran.

I was 24 when Dad left home and went his own way. The bubble had burst. Dad and Joe Pyle went out to America for a few months and were introduced to a New York mobster and his associates. When they came back to England, the cannabis from Europe, involving the Italians and the Dutch, started arriving in the UK. It would be taken to bogus fruit and veg businesses along a major A road in Kent, where they used to unload vast amounts of potatoes. Brian and Joe used it as a cover to have their cannabis delivered there. It would then be picked up and distributed on the streets of London. After a number of profitable years, this came to a sudden halt when somebody tried to steal the cargo in London. Word had it that one of the drivers got shot.

Due to the disaster, money had to be moved, so my parents met with someone in Europe to drive the outstanding money down to Italy. On arrival, not all of the money was there, so they held my mum and dad captive until Joe Pyle in London had the finances sorted. Afterwards, my mother said she had a great time – the captors had put them up in a five-star hotel. Dad wasn't too happy though, and came home with his tail between his legs.

Every once in a while, Dad and Joe would send me over to an illegal gambling den run by the Americans in the Steering Wheel Club in Shepherd Market, Mayfair. I would be given a bag and told not to look inside. I'd deliver it and the people there would give me money to take back to Dad and Joe.

Throughout all these ventures, the fear and the fearlessness in me continued to grow rapidly at the same speed, but I was beginning to achieve great heights because of my dad. Doors opened that no one could open. It was incredible, particularly as I was now the breadwinner of the family. I used to treat Mum like a queen, paying her bills and sending her on holiday. She had a good life.

On 27 October 1983, Tracy gave birth to our first child, Aimee, at Queen Charlotte's Hospital in Hammersmith. I was 25 years old. I was petrified when they first gave me my daughter. I had so much love for her, but didn't know how to filter that love. I thought it had to be spoken. I didn't realize it was an action, and so I struggled with that action. The pull of drugs, the pull of another woman, the pull of money – they all seemed easier. This love for my daughter was too pure, too clean, and too honest.

Aimee was a beautiful, peaceful baby. She never crawled, only learnt to walk. Her cot, which I bought in Harrods, was bigger than her room; I had to get her a good cot. There must have been thirty adults at her first birthday party, because I was the first one out of us to have kids.

But I became very unmanageable. I got away with it because I had money and made sure that Tracy had a good car and a good home. I used to look at Aimee and think, 'God, I love you so much.' I adored her but I couldn't get it. It didn't equate. Instead of being in the heart, it was in the head; and my heart was breaking. Tracy had got what she wanted and was the most incredible mother. Tracy's connection with her daughter Aimee made the dark in Tracy's heart become light.

To look straight and legit, I owned Upper Class Brass, a bathroom shop on Webbs Road, Wandsworth, with Edwardian and Victorian suites. One night at the shop, I had just finished cleaning taps with my mate Wayne; it was seven o'clock and we'd had a few drinks and were leaving. In his car he took apart the steering wheel, hid some cocaine inside, and put the steering wheel back together.

As I got out of his car to get into mine, I spotted a squad car going past and I saw the copper looking. I was not thinking about the coke, but the fact that I'd had a drink. Not wanting to drive, I got into Wayne's car, a red 1.4 Fiesta. As we pulled into Broomwood Road, I could see that the police were following us. I took my shoes off and put my socks on my hands, then Wayne handed me one ounce of coke.

There were one, two, three police cars chasing us now and Wayne was going extremely well. Left onto Bolingbroke Grove, straight to Wandsworth Common Station, right at the station towards Bellevue Road. We drove past new builds, smashing through gardens and fences. The police lost us for about a minute, so I threw the one ounce of coke over a big fence beside us.

Then we went into reverse. This guy sandpapering the bottom of a small boat fell off his bench as we went through his garden. I remember the shock on his face. We'd cut his fence in half.

We were now in a cul-de-sac with no way out, but there was another big fence. So we went forward and – bang – hit a concrete post. Wayne went through the windscreen and fell back down. The steering wheel was embedded in his chest and I could see the bone of his nose, with blood spurting out. I had busted my knee and ankle.

Police were everywhere. They got me out of the car. The ambulance was there, but the police didn't care. I was writhing in pain and looking at Wayne, who I thought was going to die. They found the one ounce, but they didn't find the remaining cocaine, because the car was squashed.

After they'd taken me to St George's Hospital in a wheelchair, an Indian doctor there told them, 'If he can move his knee, we can discharge him.'

'Okay. How do you get his knee to work?' the police officer responded.

'There're no breakages; he has stretched his tendons. But there's a muscle relaxer that, I suppose, within a day or two, can get it working.'

I heard the copper reply, 'He needs to leave this hospital now.'

'The only way he can leave is if his leg is straightened out, but it won't work immediately,' said the doctor.

'It has to.'

I heard the copper and swore at him. He replied, 'You ain't staying in here, mate, so you can escape. You're coming to the police station.'

The doctor came in and sprayed all around my leg, but my leg wouldn't move. 'Try a bit more,' the copper told me.

Actually I wasn't trying at all. But I said, 'I can't move it.'

The copper then went *bash!* with his hands on my knees. He said, 'It's moved.' It was naughty. They took me to Brixton police station in a wheelchair.

A few days later, after appearing in court, I was sitting in no man's land between A and B wing, waiting to go into the hospital wing. It was not a good place to be at eight o'clock at night. Then the prison officer shouted out, 'Emmett!'

I thought, 'What's happening here?'

'You've got bail,' he said. I could not believe it. Dad had worked his magic on the legal system.

With a bent passport, I managed to get out of the country and flew to Lanzarote with Tracy and Aimee. A few weeks later, they returned home to South Wimbledon. My brother Martin took care of them and they became very, very close. My daughter loved him dearly, calling him 'Mart, Mart' and he became the father figure.

Meanwhile, I went to live in Marbella and started the exploits which took me to France and Germany. Tracy and Aimee used to visit me every two months and I fell madly in love with Aimee. Every time she left, it would break my heart. Tracy was still being a great mother, protector, and dual parent. They both seemed very happy.

9. MARTIN

Marbella was hot and very romantic, with the glitz of the sun, sea, and lovely beaches. It was not ostentatious but there were nice restaurants and the people were smart. Everyone was laughing. It was wonderful and a really cool place to be – but it was at the embryonic stage of drug smuggling, and I took my chance.

I lived in an apartment on a golf course, part of a timeshare that was one of the area's first urbanizations. The lower part had really nice apartments, but the higher you got, the worse the flats were. I rented a not-so-nice one-bedroom with a pull-down settee and small bathroom, painted all white with green louvre blinds. The view was of the number-one tee, but the flat was five out of ten. Still, I was a little boy on the run from the police and the place suited me: my therapy home, where I used to sit and try to work out Michael Emmett.

I wasn't at ease with Michael. But I looked and sounded good, with all the credentials: I had an infamous father, I could pull a gal, and I was busy. But the trauma of the broken child in me was getting harder to cope with, and I would put on this villain mask. I didn't like it. I felt really out of sorts. I felt vulnerable.

In July 1985 my grandfather, John Watkins, was dying. Mum sent my brother Martin out to be with me. Martin was 21 years old and all excited, with his girlfriend Helen who was three months pregnant. I created a situation for Martin which would earn him about 1,500 quid a month to keep them going. Martin, Tracy, Helen, and I were really close – together the whole time. We used to go and see Dire Straits, try out restaurants, and get high together.

That summer, my brother and I hung out in Marbella and had some fun. There were plenty of boats, plenty of pretty girls, and plenty of wealth so, momentarily, I could live the dream. It stopped me going home and closing the door, having a joint, and thinking, 'What did I do today?'

On 29 July, Martin and I went back to my apartment. We'd had a bit of cocaine and started arguing about our dad's behaviour. There were no strikes or blows; still, it was not nice. We agreed to disagree but Martin walked out. We'd only argued about three times in our life. The night before it had been about my girlfriend Tracy. 'I really want you to love Tracy, Michael. She's a great girl,' Martin had said.

After Martin walked out, he must have got a lift because I found him far away from my flat, walking around at the bull ring in Puerto Banús with his clothes in his bag. I said, 'Get in the car. Come with me.' As I took him home, we were quiet.

Then Martin told me he needed some money. I had £1,000 in £50 notes so I gave half to him. He took the money and I went to bed. But about 10 minutes later, I heard the car leave, and there was nothing I could do.

When I woke up in the morning, I walked into the bathroom and saw that Martin had written *I luv you* on the mirror in Vaseline. I had no idea why. I was stuck, up on the hill, with no car. But eventually I got myself into town, borrowed a car, and drove everywhere looking for him. I can remember the clothes he was wearing – dressed like a monied, horsey person, with beige twill trousers, a nice-fitting blue, brown and white dogtooth gentleman's jacket which belonged to my dad, and smart brogues. I headed to Málaga airport with two young boys, the sons of my mate. The airport was small, so small that you could count the number of flights coming to and from the UK every week. It was Tuesday and I knew that the British Midland flight would have taken off that afternoon.

I asked the girl at the airport desk. 'Hi, love, can you tell me if my brother got on that flight?'

She said, 'I can't tell you anything, but we allowed someone on the flight who said that their grandfather was dying in England.' That had to be Martin, I reckoned. So I sat in Departures, waiting for 2 hours 50 minutes for the flight to arrive in England. By that time it was eight or nine o'clock at night. But when I phoned up, I was told he hadn't been on the flight.

So I drove to a bar in Port Banús and phoned up Martin's best buddy, Ted. I said, 'Has Martin turned up yet?'

'No,' he went.

'He's dead, isn't he?' I said. I don't know where that came from.

'Yes, he's dead.'

Martin had been crushed by a lorry.

I stumbled out into the car park. It was so baking hot that I couldn't move. The car park was rammed, I couldn't get out.

I said to the two young boys in my car, 'Martin's dead.' They couldn't believe it. Everything became surreal, with the anxiety and an overwhelming feeling of losing my mind. All I wanted was for the past 24 hours to change. The boys took me round to their dad and mum, who were beautiful souls.

Gradually it emerged what had happened. Martin used to drive very fast, particularly in my silly little panda car, which was like a beach chair on wheels and very dangerous. He was going along the A-45, the main road from Málaga down to Cádiz, which had a deadly reputation. On a massive bend, Martin lost control and the car flew to the other side of the road. A lorry drove over it, squashing the car and killing Martin outright.

The following day, Tracy, Dad, and Arthur Suttie arrived in Marbella. I was overwhelmed and relieved to see Tracy there as I didn't know she was coming. We went to the mortuary, a cottage-style building shaped like a fifty-pence piece, with wrought iron and blinds. It was very old Spanish – and it was closed for siesta. I could see the freezer doors where they had put Martin.

We sat down and waited.

Dad said, 'What happened? I thought it was you at first.'

I didn't even listen to him.

'How does that make you feel?' I said.

'I don't know.'

Dad then asked me, 'What did you do to him?'

'Leave him alone,' Tracy said. 'Leave him alone.'

Dad went, 'No, you killed him.'

It was horrendous.

The man in charge of the mortuary returned from

his siesta and pulled out Martin's body. I could see by the sheets that the boy was not complete. He was wrapped in a cloth; all they showed us was his left eye, his nose and half his face. There was nothing else we were allowed to see. When I bent forward to kiss him, I could taste his sweat.

I should never have moved the sheet off his face. The rest of his face was horrific. I pulled the sheet back over.

'Dad, kiss him,' I said.

'No. Get Martin out,' he replied. But Martin couldn't be taken out: my brother was in bits. Arthur and Tracy understood the situation, but Dad was under the influence of drink.

'Get my son out of that place. I want to hold him.'

It was terrible.

'Dad, stop it. Your son's dead.'

'Don't you tell me what to do. Get him out.'

'Dad, leave him. You need to leave him alone.'

Dad was trying to get the ring off his own hand and put it on Martin's finger.

'You cannot touch the body,' said the mortuary director. 'Please leave.'

Security came. Dad loved that. 'You try and throw me out,' he said.

He wouldn't listen to Arthur Suttie. Then Tracy just said, 'Brian,' and he calmed down. He always did listen to Tracy.

We gave the guy the ring and, from that moment, they sealed Martin's coffin. No one saw him again. We weren't allowed to see him in England. That was it. When I gave the guy the suit, he said, 'I can't dress him. I'll lay it on top.'

As we left, I said to the director of the mortuary, 'Would you please tell the man who drove the lorry that we've forgiven him and it's not his fault.' It just came out spontaneously, I didn't know where from. But I wanted to let the guy know that it was okay; to let him get on with his life.

That night, I was lying in bed trying to sleep and sedating myself with cannabis. Dad was drunk and got into bed with me. I could feel his beard against my face as he tried to console me.

I can remember saying, 'Dad, I need to use the toilet.' When I got out of the bed, I felt really uncomfortable. I went out of the room and when I returned half an hour later he was asleep, so I left him. In the morning, Dad started drinking again. He staggered out into the road and nearly got run over.

When we went to see the police, they gave me back £250 of the £500 I had given Martin. The notes were covered in his blood; I still have that money.

I remember Freddie Foreman and his wife Maureen coming out to console my dad. But Dad was still drunk and misbehaving. He and I had a fight in the street. Then he said, 'I'm having a heart attack, I'm having a heart attack.' The ambulance came and took him to Málaga hospital, where they did an ECG and administered some Valium.

Now I disconnected from Dad and came into my own a little bit.

I got Martin's body onto a flight with my dad and Tracy. I could see my brother's coffin on a little tripod on the tarmac. It was a beautiful Catholic oak coffin with a crucifix on top. I felt proud, safe, comfortable. 'He's on his way now.' I couldn't fly into the UK, as I was wanted by the police; neither could Arthur, because, while he'd been away helping us, he'd been stung for an operation dealing in speed – amphetamines.

So we flew from Málaga into Paris then got the train to Calais. On arrival, we saw lots of foot soldiers. We had our backpacks on and pretended to be holidaymakers. It was chock-a-block with people, which was perfect. But then we fell asleep and by the time we had reached Dover, most of the holidaymakers had left. All I could see were more foot soldiers flooding the port. I thought that was it; I thought, *Oh my god, I'm going to get nicked.*

Passport control was about twenty steps ahead of me. Seeing a lady with two children, Arthur leapt forward saying, 'Can I help you, madam?' Helping with the buggy, Arthur now had his cover, and he got through. I was the literally the last person off the boat. It felt like I was taking twenty steps to my execution. But the Customs and Excise people said, 'Hurry up, mate. Come on. We want to go.' They didn't even look at me.

I got out the other side and I was now in England. I got a taxi from Dover to Chelsea, went around to a mate's house, and opened a bottle of brandy.

There, my friend said, 'I'm really sorry about your granddad.'

I didn't know he was dead. Within three days, Martin and my grandfather John Watkins had died. We buried them on the same day.

I couldn't carry Martin's coffin; I couldn't go into the church. Martin's best friend Johnny Leach, who was a lovely man, took me in his old potato van to Mum's house. Terry Sansom, a notorious villain, then smuggled me in the boot of his Rolls-Royce and drove me to my brother's funeral. There were loads of people, because we buried Martin and my grandfather on the same day. The Kray twins sent a wreath, the Richardsons sent theirs, all the Great Train Robbers. I got out of the car boot and mingled with the crowd. No one knew I was there. A few people looked but I was so traumatized that I just stared. I couldn't even look at the crowd and, in the end, I didn't care if I got arrested. Dad's business partner Joe Pyle had put a couple of travellers with motorbikes outside so I could escape if needed.

Martin's death freaked my old man out. Dad could cope with Martin a lot better than with me, except that he felt ashamed in front of my brother. He felt no shame in front of me because he knew that I was the same as him. Martin was this beautiful, elegant child who you wouldn't want to upset.

But it wasn't only the loss of his beautiful boy; it was also the end of our family. The four of us never got over his death. We still loved each other, but it was part of the destruction of the Emmetts. We never recovered, and Dad didn't know how to deal with that.

10. HIGHS AND LOWS

Still wanted by the police, I went and hid out in a caravan down in Marlow, at Harleyford Manor, where there were mobile homes on a pretty site right along the Thames. Only Tracy knew I was there – and one other person.

A few months later, I came down to London for the Harrods winter sale. I was with two mates, Clifford and Barry; all three of us were on the run. It was not for massive crimes; I was probably the worst. I had a car but it was in someone else's name and I used to drive around in it a lot.

When we arrived at the NCP car park next door to Harrods, I had a run-in with the ticket attendant and I really gave it to him. He must have phoned the police. It was foolish of me. I was thinking we'd be all right, but someone had obviously informed on me about the car. There were a lot of grasses around.

We went into the Harrods sale, then ran into Herbie Frogg to pick up my suit. As we arrived back at the car park, the police were waiting and shouted out my name. I ran but coppers were everywhere and I got caught. They took me over to my car and handcuffed me to the door; I still had the car keys in my hand. So close, yet so far.

They took us down to Chelsea Police Station, then I was remanded in Brixton Prison.

In Brixton, I shared my cell with a mate of mine. Unbeknown to me, his girlfriend, who was not talking to him, was living with my dad's girlfriend Cathy in Ibiza. Every day, my mate would wait for a letter from his girlfriend, but she didn't write to him. We just passed the time getting stoned, drunk, and all things like that. At that time, when you were on remand, you could have a drink in prison after your visit – either a can of Stella or a little bottle of rosé. There was a small area where you could get your drink. We used to sit there like we were in the pub. It was crazy stuff.

All of a sudden, a letter came through from my cellmate's girlfriend. He had been waiting three months and was thinking that she'd left him.

'I can't read it. Will you read it out loud?' he said to me, and closed his eyes.

So I read the girlfriend's letter, which finished with *Great news, Cathy and Brian are having a baby.* I couldn't believe it, that so soon after Martin's death, my dad was having another child. My mate didn't even hear that – he was just happy that his girlfriend hadn't left him. Meanwhile I was fuming about my dad.

A few months later the day came for me to be sentenced. At Brixton, any inmate who was going to court would be woken up early for breakfast, then get taken to reception. On my way over to be signed out, there was a lot of noise because Brian Reader, who went on to be the Hatton Garden robbery ringleader, and his associate Kenny Noye were going to court. They were surrounded by a ring of police. Reader suddenly popped his head out and said to me, 'Are you Brian's son?'

Reader asked the policeman to move out of the way and then he came and sat down beside me. He could see the look of fear on my face. I was looking at five years. I wasn't frightened of going to prison; I was frightened of the unknown, not being in control. I was very spoilt and always wanted my own way.

'How are you?' he said. 'You okay? Because you look a bit worried.'

'I am worried.'

'Look at the sort of trouble we're in. You'll be all right. There's nothing they can do to you.' I felt better, and Brian Reader's words sent me on my way.

In the end, I was sentenced for 18 months because I got four 'Not Guilties'. The fear of going to Wandsworth Prison was unbelievable. Wandsworth was a naughty prison where people got stabbed on the yard or had sugar and hot water thrown over them. I was so concerned and nervous that it made me ill.

From Wandsworth I was moved to Eastchurch Prison in Kent. There I continued taking drugs, and I had a couple of fights, showing the brave man in me, but also the coward. Mum and Dad came to visit me and I said to Mum, 'Can you get a cup of tea or coffee?' to get her to leave us alone at the table. Then I stared at Dad – taking my power back – and said, 'I hear you're having a baby.'

'How do you know?' my dad replied.

'It doesn't matter how I know. My brother's just died and my mother's distraught. You're having a baby. If you don't tell her, then I will.'

'I'll kill you.'

I replied, 'Do what you like. I don't care.'

Eventually, Dad told my mum about this other child. My mother was devastated. It broke her and ruined our beautiful family.

By now, Tracy was seven months pregnant with our second child, Lillie, but the prison asked her to stop visiting because there was no hospital if she went into labour. Realizing that was my ticket out of there, I put a note in to the governor requesting a transfer. It was very unusual to be granted one, but a nearby prison had been burnt down; inmates were being moved out, and some of them were coming to Eastchurch. So to make room for the new prisoners, I was put on the bus down to Ford Prison, right near Littlehampton in Sussex.

Ford's design was based on a prisoner-of-war camp with a main building and huts, but I found it more like a Butlin's holiday camp. Celebrities were in there – Georgie Best and all that. Bright and breezy, there was a lovely cricket green and you could play bowls, football, backgammon, and chess. There was the infamous Joey Wilkins and Morrie the Head, a major jewel thief, who both knew my dad.

Everyone had to work in the jail. There were some brilliant jobs, but I had the worst, doing the collars and buttonholes for the prison officers' shirts. I hated it. Every week I would put job applications in and wait patiently, but I never, ever got a job change. They'd say, 'You're lucky to be here.' So I used to just get on with it – and still managed to get involved in quite a few antics.

During my time at Ford, I became friends with the

prison chaplain, Mr Vicars, and decided to get confirmed. We used to do Bible studies and be allowed out on Sundays to go in the church warden's van to the little church in Littlehampton. There were about twelve of us in the confirmation group. Some of us were Christians, others weren't.

Beautiful Lillie was born on 25 July 1986 when I was in Ford. I'd had a fight with a black guy that same day, which took the cream off the occasion. My dad had come to visit and tell me the news. I was elated about Lillie, but the joy was overshadowed as I was nervous about being thrown out because of the fight.

Tracy left hospital very quickly to come and be with me. She introduced me to Lillie, who was only two days old, but I was preoccupied about securing what I needed inside to keep me going. Feeling that I was disregarding Lillie, Tracy got really upset with me. It was very, very hard not connecting with the love that I had for my children. I knew what was right and what was wrong, but my attitude towards everything was naughty.

Shortly afterwards I got out on appeal, and I went round to see Tracy. However, it just wasn't right with us. I could see that Tracy held my attitude towards Lillie against me. It was really difficult. Tracy thought I was all about Aimee, but I wasn't. I was besotted with Aimee but adored Lillie too. When she was a newborn, it was just very difficult to see her in prison during the visits, and also very hard to show my feelings in a place like that.

The day after I was released, I was meant to be getting confirmed. I'd been out only 24 hours. Mr Vicars phoned up Tracy's dad Harry and they got talking because they had both been military men in the war. My father-in-law had fought in the Punjab. He was a beautiful man and an incredible human being.

Harry came to me. 'I've had Mr Vicars on the phone,' he said. 'You're getting confirmed tonight at Ford Prison.'

'Harry, I don't want to do that. I'm out of there now.'

'Son, that man fought for king and country. So did I. The only thing we've got is our word. He's given me his word. You get back there and you get confirmed, son.' Harry was a real moral man.

'I don't want to.'

'You go,' Harry said. 'Do the right thing.'

That evening, a dear friend of mine drove me and Tracy to prison. The three of us arrived with a gift for my fellow inmates and friends inside. For security reasons, an inmate had to be back in prison by a certain time, and when we arrived at the prison they thought I was just coming in late. They didn't realize that I was free; it had only been 24 hours since I'd got out on appeal.

'What are you doing here, Emmett?' said one of the prison officers.

I said, 'Michael, not Emmett.'

'You're late coming back.'

'I'm not.'

'What are you doing?' he said, before asking other officers, 'Is Emmett late?'

I said, 'It's Michael.'

This prison officer, Mr Thoroughgood, had been trying to get me for six months. He didn't like me at all; he deemed me a total scallywag.

I said, 'I got released. Forget Emmett; my name is

Michael. I'm not a prisoner no more; I've been set free. I'm not on parole – the sentence got acquitted. Are you all right with that?'

He was livid.

I said, 'I've come to be confirmed.'

'What?' He didn't like that.

Tracy and I went in.

Inside, people didn't know that I'd gone home either. 'All right, Mike?' they said. 'You had a good day?' I told them I'd been released and they asked what on earth I was doing back there.

After I had been confirmed, Mr Vicars asked if I'd like a visit with my mates.

I said, 'Yes, thank you, Mr Vicars. Can my Tracy stay?'

My mates were waiting. They knew what I was going to do. I gave the gift very quickly and privately, so my friends could enjoy the rest of the evening. We returned to church and had a cup of tea and cake.

'That was quick,' said Mr Vicars.

'I just wanted to say hello, goodbye, nice to see you, and all that,' I said.

We'd done what we had to do. Now I was on alert, because when you've done something wrong in prison, you're not about to have a laugh. You've got to be on point, you've got to be focused. But everyone seemed cool: job successful.

The next day, I went to see my brother Martin's son Charles, who had been born while I was in prison. His mum Helen, who was a bit wild, was going out with one of Martin's friends, and I found the relationship difficult. But that was the way her devastation was working itself out.

Now I tried to get my life on the straight and narrow. I invested in a flower shop on Old Church Street with this Turkish guy called Ralph, who was short, fat, and hairy, with a beard and blue eyes. Ralph's father was a very wealthy man and owned clubs in the West End, where all the rich Arabs used to go. Ralph was the oldest son, but his younger brother Darren was the heir to the throne, which caused upset. Ralph began to rebel against his father.

Ralph's dad also owned a house opposite Harrods, where the Turks, Greeks, and Arabs used to play cards. We would go over there and mess around. One night, Ralph and the boys were there taking ecstasy, which my dad had just introduced into the UK – the first ecstasy ever to enter the country in the mid-Eighties. After everyone had left later that night, Ralph apparently went to one of the cupboard drawers and got out a big tin of glossy white Dulux paint, a paint roller, and a paint tray. He was very high, and he painted the whole flat white – including the furniture.

But Ralph was one of the best florists in London. He imported Dutch flowers long before anyone else, and he also had Christmas trees for sale. I became his partner, and he took me out to Germany to buy some Christmas trees. When we got there, it turned out he owed the geezer five grand – something I knew nothing about. We bought these trees and transported them back to the UK, but we got stopped at Customs because my name was on them. The Customs men drilled holes in all of them looking for drugs. The trees were duff anyway. Ralph got his money back; I suffered.

However good he was as a florist, Ralph had bad money-management skills. Eventually he became very disgruntled with the mere fact that he had two partners, which was eating into the profits. When he realized he couldn't do what he wanted, he tried to get me off the pitch.

He came to me and said, 'I've got a new staff member who's just come out of prison for manslaughter.' It was a veiled threat. Ralph didn't want me to have the stall.

'Oh, has he?'

'We've got to think about this business,' he continued.

'Okay, I'll go and see him.'

It turned out to be my mate Tony, who I'd spent time with in Ford Prison. Only young but with white hair, he'd been arrested for manslaughter after someone got stabbed in a crowd. As soon as Tony saw me, Ralph's plan was thwarted.

One day, Tony and I were just finishing up at the flower pitch when a guy called Bryn turned up. Bryn was one of the top boys at Arsenal and soon we became best mates. He was younger than me and a bit of a protégé. I looked after and guided him in the Chelsea way of life. Bryn looked like Action Man; strong, fit, and handsome. We all used to hang out in a pub on Burdett Road in East London

But the breakdown in my relationship with Ralph continued – and became hugely apparent. Ralph appeared with someone who tried to intimidate me. It ended in tears. The destruction had started.

One of Ralph's debts was attached to the wife of Howard Marks' business partner. Ralph had had a loan from her to help his business. I wasn't aware of this when I purchased my shares. These people would come down each month for Ralph to pay them some money. It was another situation where Ralph was not allowed to do what he wanted. He wanted me to get the blame for his own debts.

Ralph went to Charlie Kray for help getting out of the situation, hoping Charlie would send some heavies round to threaten me. Instead, Charlie, who had a soft spot for my family, phoned up my father and told us, and Ralph's plot failed.

In the end Ralph decided to sell his own shares in the business to part of my family, then he left and joined the circus as a fire-eater. Although we had our differences, he was very dear to me.

Not long after Ralph's departure, I was at a party when I bumped into Jane, the girlfriend of a good mate of mine, Johnny. Our families had known each other for ages. Jane and I first met at her eighteenth birthday party and we had a connection. She was a wonderful lady, very attractive and loyal. I had a deep love for her.

Even though we knew our boundaries, the connection at her eighteenth was rekindled and we found ourselves in a predicament that was dishonest; a situation where we betrayed those people closest to us. The only way this was ever going to end was in tears, so Jane quickly moved to Cornwall to get away. We went back and forth for a few years. Johnny was a good guy, very handsome and good to be around, but he and I had an altercation which got very heated and didn't end well.

Tracy was devastated by the affair but, on 16 June 1988, she gave birth to our third daughter. Beth was perfect in every way. When she was born, she flew out of her mother. That was her personality. At first, she looked like the ugly duckling, but within a year she turned into a beautiful swan. For the early years of her life, I had a lot of fun with Beth. She brought so much joy to my heart.

Yet despite the joy, the sabotage continued to soar. I was destroying everything that was good because I didn't feel good enough. I hated what I had done with Jane. I had repeated the feelings behind the sexual abuse – someone close to me, someone dangerous, and the buzz of *Was I going to get caught?*

I covered the dysfunction in my life with drink, drugs, women and money, but it was horrible. What I was doing in response to my own brokenness freaked me out. I'd sit indoors on my own for two or three days smoking cannabis, then go out and have a fight. It was insanity.

In 1989, I had a breakdown. I couldn't breathe; I was overwhelmed; hated myself. It was horrendous. Tracy, who is as kind, beautiful, and loyal as the day is long, helped me with Valium and nursed me for six months. However, I was in trouble, drinking about four pints of beer daily just to get through life.

I never let my three daughters see me in this state. I used to go to the pub to get drunk and stoned. Other times I'd go up to Epsom, completely out of it, and cry over Martin's grave before falling asleep in the cemetery. In the end, instead of me crying about Martin, I used it as an excuse to cry about myself, trying to get rid of the sadness within me. I'd then come back home and be jovial for half an hour before Tracy would put me to bed. I'd sleep until the following morning. I had a huge amount of cocaine, but it wasn't for financial gain. I needed it for my own fix.

Meanwhile, Dad and Joe Pyle were on remand for a ton of puff – cannabis resin. One summer's night in 1989, Dad turned up in this little blue van at our little house in Sutton. He had just been acquitted and had walked out on Cathy and their new baby Alice. He said, 'I've lost everything.'

So I let him come and live with us, but Dad was a slippery man. He had lots of money and dug a hole in my garden underneath the pond to hide his cash. One day, it rained and some of the money got wet. He brought out about £20,000 and put the notes in the oven to warm it up, then went upstairs. Tracy came in, saw the oven was on low and turned it up. My dad came running downstairs just in time.

It was mad, yet Dad was happy because he was back with his family. Tracy and my children were very close to my little nephew Charles, so his mum Helen often dropped him round. He was Martin's double and became like a surrogate brother to my daughters. Then Dad met a young psychiatric nurse Rosheen, who lived around the corner from us and they started seeing each other. But Tracy and I parted ways.

After the break-up, Dad came to me one night. 'I've got an idea,' he said. 'Do you want to go out to Spain?' He knew I was always game for anything; I had fire in my belly. So Dad and I started hatching a plan to smuggle a massive load of puff. Within a month, I had arrived in Marbella.

We worked well together. Dad was the brains; I was the quick thinker. He could do *The Times* crossword; I struggled with the *Beano* crossword. Dad was intelligent and would always take time to think about things. I would make decisions on my feet, some of which were incredibly good but others incredibly bad.

A few months later after I'd arrived, I was hanging out with my mate Adam and we decided to go to a brothel. I wasn't really into women of the night, but we'd been using cocaine. In the end, nothing happened. The Maastricht Treaty had devalued the pound so the pound was useless and they wouldn't accept our money.

So we drove back to our hotel to get out some cash. As I got out of the car, there were four girls standing on the steps of the hotel casino. I was stoned and trying to steady myself, putting one foot in front of the other. I suddenly looked up and saw this girl, Daniella. I was smitten and fell in love with her instantly.

The next week I took Daniella out to dinner. I ate suckling pig; she had veal. We kissed goodnight. Several days later, she decided that she really liked me. We slept with each other and went swimming; and within two weeks we had moved in together. We had a beautiful four-bedroom house in the hills. It was nothing glam, but built well in a Moroccan style by a Jewish guy. There was a minstrel gallery, tiles everywhere, and glass doors ornately engraved with roses. Our relationship wasn't based on sex or drugs. She knew the naughty stuff I was doing, but we loved everything about each other. It was like we'd known each other for years. It was really strange.

But my crime was intensifying. Now I started smuggling heavily from Morocco to the UK.

11. A DONE DEAL

One day, through a Moroccan connection, I was approached by a Buddhist called Dennis Lemonnier. Six-feet-two tall, fat as a chip, and very Basque, he had dreadlocked hair like a Jamaican and bushy black eyebrows with dandruff in them. Dennis was the cleverest and most compassionate of men, although with the worst table manners. He loved the minerals from the earth and was into organic growth of anything, be it people, fruit, or vegetables.

Dennis lived up in the hills in Marbella. He used to come and visit me once a month in his beaten old car, which had one blue door and one yellow. We would meet in very out-of-the-way places, where he'd walk in looking like he'd just slept in his clothes, with one collar up and one collar down. Daniella used to say, 'Has he bathed?'

Dennis, who knew the smuggling game inside out, would come to me and say, 'They want you to get the cannabis into the UK.'

To Dennis, cannabis was just an organic plant that grew, and he chilled out with it. He understood the growth of the stuff. In his mind, growing mint, cauliflower, or a potato was virtually the same as growing cannabis. We would talk; then, as Dennis left, he would give me a small bag of homegrown grass.

'This is good. Be careful,' he'd say.

From there, things began to develop. Dennis Lemonnier was the mouthpiece and became the bridge between me and a huge drug-smuggling outfit in Morocco. I started meeting Italians, Bosnians, but the big one was a boy who lived in Holland. He was part of a dangerous gang that would kill you if they had to. They were the money people and always wanted a huge amount of cash.

I had been told that the cocaine would be put in big cigar-like tubes then sealed and a magnet would be attached. The tubes would be dropped from a low aircraft into the sea in South America, where the magnet would attach to merchant ships. When one of the ships reached international waters, where you couldn't be arrested, it would drop the gear there. The smugglers would then get people to go lobster-potting or deep-sea diving, to pull up the gear into their little fishing boats and bring it to shore.

My father was approached by the organization, asking if we could assist in landing a boat-load of cannabis, off the coast of Africa. It was dropped in February 1993 in the Bristol Channel. There was an Eastern-European guy in the gang. I called him Bert the Bastard. He was a lunatic and wore the biggest crucifix around his neck. The night before the drop, when we were staying in a Welsh hotel, Bert took his crucifix off and said, 'This boat-load of cannabis is a gift from God. We share this, do this, and everything is okay'. Bert was quite aggressive in his approach and he was concerned for the security of the cannabis because we weren't the owners.

I said, 'Don't worry about it, Bert.'

The following day, the gear arrived. Apparently an HMS ship steamed towards the boat and towed it into harbour. It became obvious that Customs and Excise were suspicious so they aborted the millions of pounds' worth of cannabis at sea.

Me and Bert went to the harbour. This was a Customs-controlled port so I warned him, 'Bert, don't go through the main gate.' He walked in, while I climbed over the fence with a hoodie and gloves on, and a scarf over my mouth.

We approached the three guys and the captain on the boat.

Bert told the captain, 'There'll be consequences.'

He replied, 'Bert, Bert.' Then he appealed to me, 'Say something, Michael.' I didn't say anything; I was just shocked.

But Bert and I went on our way. In the darkness of the night, tails between our legs and disappointed, we scampered to our car, parked 2 miles from the harbour.

Then, on the M5 coming out of Wales, a squad car with two Welsh coppers pulled me onto the hard shoulder. I got out of my car and walked to the police car. The coppers said I was speeding, but I knew I wasn't. The hairs went up on the back of my neck.

They asked for my details. I wondered about giving the wrong name, but then thought that could cause me more problems if they took me to the police station and fingerprinted me. Thinking there was no evidence so they couldn't nick me, I calmed down: maybe it was a routine check. So I decided to give my name and they allowed me to go back to the car. Then they asked to see Bert's passport, and we passed it out of the small opening in the window without looking at them. They gave it back and we drove off.

I felt I'd slipped the net again, knowing full well that no arrest would have been made by a squad car. Suspicion in my head was 50/50 but, again, I dismissed it. After I took Bert to the airport, I never saw him again. I never knew his real name, but he was a real strong man with guts; a man I liked and respected.

Just before I flew back to Spain, a known fence in Chelsea told a friend of mine, 'Tell Michael they're onto him badly'. Unbeknown to Bert and me, the surveillance at the harbour had been intense and Customs had been taking photographs. So when I returned to Marbella, I downed tools on the Morocco drugs operation and took it easy. I was aware that I had been playing a dangerous game.

Seven months later, Dennis Lemonnier approached me and my dad and asked, 'Do you want to do it again?' We said yes and started to develop a plan.

Twice a year, due to sea conditions, a huge consignment of grown hashish left Pakistan, which had a street value of £1.8 million per ton. In Pakistan, hashish only cost £50 a kilo. The expenditure was transport. The gear was smuggled in among cargo on a grandmother ship, a mother ship, and a daughter ship. The locations were all around the world's seas, with distribution points in Canada, Australia, Italy, and France, which was the toughest. Then it came to England – our patch.

Just before I left for England, I went to meet these Moroccan guys on the beach in Marbella. For security,

Dad was watching me from a beach house, although I didn't know it. Dad was so slippery and cunning, like a rat up a drainpipe.

On the beach, the guys told me, 'We're going to put 250 kilos of cocaine on with the cannabis.'

'All right,' I said. 'That's fine.' I knew it could be sneaked in nicely that way, and a kilo of coke was worth thirty grand. If I did it, they told me, I could have 125 kilos of cocaine for myself, which would have earned a few million quid.

I left the beach and, as I was getting into my car, I heard the infamous whistle. My dad was there. He said, 'Someone took a photograph of you.' But I didn't really listen and just headed home.

As I was going up the hill, I saw Daniella in the distance; she seemed to be crying. I tried to catch up with her but then saw this guy I knew. He was standing by the phone booth.

'You're going back to London, aren't you?' he asked me.

Wondering how he could know, I replied, 'Yes, I am.'

'What are you going back for?'

'To have my teeth done. Anyway, gotta go.'

I felt uneasy; something inside me was triggered. I couldn't find Daniella anywhere, but I felt inspired to drive back to the beach.

When I got there, I said to the Moroccan guys, 'Don't put the cocaine on with the cannabis.'

'Why, why?' they asked.

But I insisted, 'Just don't put it on.' I had a sixth sense that the cocaine shouldn't go on there – and also that we should kill the entire deal.

But I didn't do that; I was in it to win it.

I flew home, but I should never have left Daniella. Although I had three children with Tracy, Daniella was now the woman I loved, and she loved me. Daniella understood me, understood what I used to go through. She was an incredible woman who had done her utmost to keep me in a very comfortable environment.

When I got back to the UK, everything was ready. All the meetings and coordinates were done. Security was very tight. We had nicknames and a voicemail system in Paris. If I wanted to speak to someone, I would send them a bleep, then ring the voicemail in Paris and leave a message, which came out as a Donald Duck voice. I'd say, 'Meet me at rendezvous four.' Then they would delete it. If we gave out a phone number, we subtracted ten from every number.

Dad told me not to go. We had done our bit, he said. But greed, plus the urge for control and the lure of stardom, took over me.

On Friday, 5 November 1993, Alan Trotter and I drove slowly from London to Bideford on the Devon coast. Alan was a bank robber, who tended to get freaked out. He had been in prison for a long time and had been taking acid. When Alan was released, he had started using class-A drugs, got himself into a terrible state, and distanced himself from everybody. When he recovered, people found it hard to believe he was the man he used to be. After a while, I'd seen that he was on the mend. He was clean and sober and I loved him dearly, as I had known him since he was six. He was my driver. He wasn't hands-on, but we had certain vehicles that used to transport the money.

Alan had also been out in Spain with me and he would assist with the guys who used to babysit our product.

Now we were staying for the next three nights in a beautiful Devon farmhouse, which was also the hub for the English part of the Morocco operation. The farmhouse was owned by Peter Bracken, my partner, who had also worked with Dad on and off. Ten years older than me, Peter was like a Sixties' drug child. Blond, blue-eyed, and bow-legged, with a haircut like the teen pop idol David Cassidy, he looked a bit like part of the New Zealand rugby team. When Peter and I were talking, there was always a third person in the room – his ego. Our relationship was hard, a challenge, because he loved my dad and was jockeying for position.

We arrived in Bideford as the pub was closing, but we still went and had a jolly-up. I got a bit of cocaine off the local lad and we went to Peter's house, three or four miles down the road outside the town. One of our rules and regulations was that we were never stoned or drunk during a deal. It didn't always work out like that, but that was the intention. Although I'd had a couple of lines of coke, I had my serious mind about me as I told Peter what I thought we should do.

I wasn't nervous; I was taking it full-on. But I could tell that Alan Trotter was nervous. Alan was lovely and loyal, but very much a rabbit caught in the headlights. He was also tired, and he went to bed.

I sat up with Peter Bracken, and I could see that he wanted me to stay in Bideford rather than go home. He knew I was game; I was never fearful of doing crime. I didn't care, nor had much real grasp of the consequences. I'd usually go, 'Sod it, this is going to be all right.' My fearlessness was boundless; it was beyond belief. It was not because I was a brave man; I just did what I did. Thinking on my feet is what I was good at, but to get the best results I had to activate my mind, otherwise it could be quite lethargic. I was a multiplicity of emotions: there were about nine people living in Michael, and they all had their little heads. It was crazy.

Waking up on Saturday morning with hangovers, Alan, Peter, and I spent the day mooching about Peter's house. There was nothing worse than having a cocaine hangover after drinking brandy, but we all had a little smoke and cooked some nice pork. It was a big house so enough space to be on our own, read the paper, and keep a lookout. But now my brain was starting: I stepped up to the plate and started making plans.

Yet I was still asking myself whether I wanted to go home. Dad called and told me, 'Don't you dare stay.'

I thought, *Why am I staying? Is it greed?*

Tired out, I decided to nip away on the Sunday before the drugs arrived at Bideford in the evening. I could see Peter wanted me there and was trying to be friendly with me so I'd stay on. But I had met my side of the bargain safely and earnt my cut; now it was his turn. Peter had guts and he was very game and trustworthy, so I was confident he could pull it off.

I was on edge and feeling wary. I was trying to remember the little bits of information which I had received about Police and Customs over the last nine months. Then a couple of cars pulled up at Peter's farmhouse, including Fred, who was the transport, and Tony Rutherford, the fishmonger, who was going to collect the consignment.

As we went into the town, some travellers started talking to Peter.

I asked him, 'Is that geezer there all right?'

Peter said, 'Oh, he's been there for two or three weeks. You want to have a look at him?'

He didn't look like a traveller; something wasn't right with the guy; he was too foreign. But I dismissed it.

At one o'clock the captain of our boat, a proper old Devon man called Dick Fishley, emerged from the local pub. He was still meant to be at sea.

Peter and I walked over to him. Dick said, 'It's on the beach over there.'

We looked where he was indicating. The drugs had already arrived – but twelve hours early, on the daytime tide rather than during the night. Just five tons of cannabis out of the full hundred had been unpacked. The tide had now gone out and the boat was stuck in the sand off Bideford, with the rest of the cannabis still on board.

'We'll have to wait for the water to come up and lift the boat. Then we can unload,' said Dick.

I was over my hangover, clean-shaven, teeth brushed, and hair washed. I was itching to go. I didn't like the situation and decided to leave.

'You can't leave,' said Peter. 'You've got to come and help me'

'I've done my job. I want to go home. I've got the cannabis here. This is your end of it.'

'You should stay with me,' he said again.

'I don't want to. I've done my work.'

I called the phone system in Paris and activated the code. Both Dennis Lemonnier and my dad responded.

They heard me say in the Donald Duck voice, 'Sweet', which they found confusing because the message wasn't due until midnight. It was still only two o'clock on Sunday afternoon.

But now, despite my plan to leave and all my protests to Peter, I had begun to think the danger had passed. Dick was there; no one had been nicked. So I stayed after all, and helped to organize the next bit.

Time flew by that day. Before I knew it, it was five o'clock in the afternoon and Peter was saying, 'Oh, come on, mate, let's get going.'

But by now my criminal mind was involved again. It was, 'All right, move that. Put that there. Don't do that. Make sure he's all right. Let's get on, let's do it.' I couldn't help myself; I was a control freak.

Alan Trotter said to me, 'I thought we was going home.'

'You rest,' I told him. 'We're going to be all right.' Then I said, 'Peter, I'm staying.'

As day turned to night, security had gone completely out the window. Mentally, I was already counting the money, and I began to make a few arrangements.

'What about parking my car up on the hill?' Peter suggested, to get a good view of the harbour.

'Do you know what, mate? I think we'll be all right,' I replied, because the gear had already been there for six hours. The truck collecting the drugs was going to go over to Torquay. I was feeling really cool about the whole situation.

Then the phone went with an alert that we had a voicemail message. 'That ain't right, mate.' I said. There was nothing on the voicemail.

Our transport, Fred, wouldn't pick up the phone. When our call was eventually answered, the signal on the new big-brick Motorola mobile phones wasn't good.

I was suspicious now. 'Something's gone on. What's happened there, mate?' I asked Peter.

'Mike, you know how them phones are like. They lose their battery charge.' Peter, I realized, was numb to the situation; he knew there was no backing out. It was an alert, and I thought to myself, *I don't have to be here.* But Peter was my pal and partner.

Finally I decided we would just take a slow little drive through Bideford to check on how the operation was going.

I said, 'Alan, get ready, mate. Let's check it out. Take your time. Drive through slowly. Let's have a little look at this.'

The tide had come in and the boat was afloat in the harbour. In the meantime, Dick and his guys had set up the tripod and harness, with a big yellow container attached. The yellow container would be swung back and forth from the boat, picking up and dropping off the gear. The fishmonger Tony Rutherford was waiting on the quayside with his big freezer van, full of frozen cod to hide the drugs in, ready to receive and transport the haul to Torquay. The team started to move the cannabis.

Suddenly halogen lights went on. It was Customs and Excise. They read Dick and the other guys their rights and arrested everyone.

None of us in the car knew what had happened, even though I was filled with suspicions. As we approached the lovely small brick bridge into Bideford, I said, 'Slow down,

Alan, slow down.' But it was quiet, dead quiet, and I said, 'It seems all right.' The road narrowed as we went over the bridge, where there was only enough room for one car. I looked for the boat, the truck, and the fishmonger, but couldn't see anything.

The next moment, a black VW Golf came tearing towards us out of the darkness. I thought we were driving on the wrong side of the road. Alan said, 'No, we're not.' Then they put on the police light on top of the car. Armed officers jumped out. We were trapped.

A megaphone blasted out, 'Michael Emmett, don't move! Get down on your knees.'

12. THE MUSTARD SEED

When I was arrested by armed officers in Bideford, my old life ended and my new life began.

I'd had enough of crime. Everybody involved in the deal was caught, including Dad, Peter Bracken, and Dennis Lemonnier. I had thought our plan in Bideford was really good and that Dad was safe where he was, staying at a hotel in Brighton, to be well out of the way when the drugs arrived in Bideford. But he had been nicked there, and I was gutted. He had also been injured when being chased by the police.

As soon as I saw him, my immediate urge was to protect him. I had every emotion possible for the man: a level of hatred and love; a level of disrespect and respect.

The coppers put me in the cells in Barnstaple police station, but I didn't give them anything. After a day and a half, Billy Boyd, the Customs man, turned up at my cell.

'Look, Michael, what stuck out for me is two things,' he said. 'One, you wept. Two, you're the only person in this police station who hasn't given me their name or address. I need to know.'

I said, 'You know my name and you know where I live. I wept about my kids, mate.'

'And I respect that,' he said. 'Now, do you want to speak to your kids?'

'Yes, I wouldn't mind.'

'No one's had a phone call in here yet, but I'll give you one if you tell me your name and address so I can formally charge you. Your dad's given us his name and address, but he hasn't told us anything else.'

He let me have a phone call and I was charged for drug importation.

Alan Trotter was being let go, but he was refusing to leave. He said to me, 'If I go, your dad will have me killed outside.'

I said, 'What are you talking about? He's not going to kill you. You need to leave.'

Eventually Alan left, but his life was never the same afterwards. Everyone thought that he'd opened his mouth, but he never. He was a good, honourable friend.

Meanwhile, Peter, Dennis, Dad, and I, plus the eight others involved in the drop, were taken to Exeter Prison, which was dark and violent. Made of Victorian brick, the prison cells were bright – but not bright nice. They were bright uncomfortable, painted suicide blue. The bed was horrible. It was hard, all metal, and had nothing to create a warm environment with.

There was a heroin epidemic there. Heroin was fairly new on the scene and people didn't know the consequences of heroin use, so the boys in the prison were robbing and cutting each other. There was a history of suicides too, with five boys having taken their own lives over the previous six months.

At the prison there were the Welsh boys, who were really

tough, and the Plymouth guys, who were a bit odd. Since we were close to the port, a number of the prisoners were sailors. There were also about five or six London groups. But when we came along, we took control of the prison. Not by being forceful, just because of who they thought we were – and a number of people had heard of Dad.

I shared a cell with my old man, who was the oldest inmate in the prison. He'd say, 'Roll me a joint, son,' and then sit on his bed in front of his easel and paint. Dad was a good technical drawer; then he went into more colourful and bold art, starting in crayon, then moving onto oil. His paintings were colourful with houses, water, and trees. There was always sunshine in my dad, but sadly it was something that he couldn't totally develop.

After the second joint, Dad was gone. Bizarrely, considering the amount of cannabis he'd been involved with, this was the first time he'd ever got high. He used to sing Irish ballads out of the windows and I loved it.

A week later we appeared in court. We were transported in the prison van along the A361, a very long road which was cleared to make way for us. I was shocked. It was very intense, as if they were moving the IRA, with helicopters, guns, and bullet-proof vests. The thing is your ego can give you loads of confidence, but in the cold light of day, the fear is, 'What is going on here?' The high level of security was down to Dennis and his connections to the organization – in case anyone tried to spring him from custody.

They took us to Barnstaple Crown Court and all we heard was, 'Bail refused'. I remember the guy in the court had a funny accent.

Afterwards, we returned to Exeter Prison. The level of security continued to be unbelievable. One day, after I hurt my ankle playing football, four armed officers accompanied me to Exeter Hospital in a prison van. It had changed from two prison officers being really cool and getting a cab.

Two of the officers said, 'You can have eggs and bacon in the café, but don't run away.'

'I can't run anywhere,' I said. I was even chained to the X-ray machine.

When I was back on my feet, I continued the job I'd been doing at the prison gym. I would get up at six or seven in the morning, have a joint, then go for breakfast downstairs, where all the inmates would be walking around robotically with their food on metal trays. I usually had porridge with honey. Some days I had a boiled egg with sausage, and wafer-thin bacon curled up like a pig's tail on a piece of fried bread. There were piles of bread and you were always encouraged to take several slices.

After breakfast, I headed over to the gym, where sometimes I would stay all day. Peter Bracken was also a gym orderly, along with Ian Hall and John Morgan, lovely guys from East London. The job included putting everyone's tracksuits in the washing machine and tumble dryer but, to make sure my tracksuit didn't shrink, I never did that with mine. I used to hand-wash it and leave it to dry on a hanger at the end of my cell.

One day, Peter and I were playing badminton. It was a hot day so we took our tracksuit tops off. I saw Peter look at my top, jealous that mine hadn't shrunk in the wash. Just before we were about to start the game, a prison officer came round shouting that we needed to put our names inside our clothes. When we finished the game, I went over to find my top had gone and that Peter had run off. I went and found him. He had picked up my top, knowing full well it was mine, and run into his office and put his name in it with a marker pen.

I said, 'Peter, that's my top.'

'No, it's not, it's mine,' he said and walked off.

The next day, I decided to organize a round-robin game of badminton. There were four of us, including Peter. I knew I was good at badminton and Peter liked to beat me. Peter was good too, but he suffered from asthma. Peter was wearing my tracksuit. I refused to put his on.

After the second game, I'd got Peter. I did overhead shots so he had to come to the net, then I'd knock them over his head. I was not scoring points; I was just wearing him out. He didn't realize what I was doing. There were only a couple of points between us. In the end, I let him win and was out of the game. Wandering over to the side of the court where Peter had taken off my tracksuit top, I took it back, rushed into the office, wrote my name in it with a marker pen in bigger letters, and put it on. Then I got Peter's tracksuit top and put his name in that.

By now, Peter had realized what had happened and came storming over.

'You've got my shirt.'

I replied, 'No, I haven't. Yours is on the floor.'

'That's not mine.'

Pointing to the top I was now wearing, I said, 'This one did have your name on it. I've scrubbed it off and put my name in it.'

Peter came running at me. He was a big strong boy but I flipped to one side and smashed him right in the head. Peter got hold of me and threw me against the wall.

Someone went and got my dad, who was in the shower, but came running in. I was looking for something on the prison officer's desk to smack Peter with.

'Peter, put him down,' Dad told him.

Peter turned around. 'Brian, I thought you were on my side.'

I just went, 'Oh really?' But I remember walking back to my cell so upset.

Dad and I had a bad argument about it. Historical stuff would always come out in my anger; I used to bring up things from when I was younger and tell him what he'd done.

He'd go, 'Stop it, stop it.' He was in total denial about head-butting me and all sorts of things.

I remember saying to him one day, 'You're just like your dad. The devil on two sticks.'

He freaked. 'Please don't say that to me.'

Most days, I had visitors. I was a bit of a fashion freak and liked to look my best for my visits, with a pair of cords, Stone Island jumper and nice trainers. I used to have a massive sugar rush because my visitors would always bring food: steak sandwiches, Kentucky Fried Chicken, and sweet stuff. They used to sneak it in.

Other times, I would get hold of some fresh chicken and a kettle. I'd cook the chicken by using the electricity from the light. I would put the hot water in the kettle then put a metal cereal bowl on top of the element before putting margarine in the bowl and cooking whatever I wanted.

But sometimes I was stuck with prison food. I loved the fish and chips on Fridays because I made fish-and-chip sandwiches. Then there were curries, pilchards on toast, and plenty of stews. On Sundays, we'd have a roast, which would be fried potatoes and packet beef, or a quarter of a chicken. We always had a duff (pudding) like Jam roly-poly, custard with skin on top, or semolina with jam.

Everyone was banged away at 8 p.m. In the early days of sharing a cell, Dad was very difficult, but I didn't see a lot of him after he got a job at reception, one of the best jobs in the prison. They loved Dad at reception because he did great work organizing the big wooden shelves where the boxes of prisoners' belongings were stored. Dad would leave our cell at 7 a.m. and wouldn't get back till 11 p.m., so we weren't locked up at the usual 8 p.m. We took full advantage of the open-door policy. When Dad returned, I used to sneak out onto the landing with him, hide behind his legs, and make a late-night phone call.

Meanwhile Daniella was like a knight in shining armour. She was totally devastated when I got arrested. It ruined her life. A beautiful lady, Daniella was like Mother Teresa and showed me unconditional love. She visited me every day, five days a week, for eighteen months – from London to Exeter. She wrote to me every day too. She was everything, and everyone loved her.

Daniella was desperate for me to finish my sentence. She adored me and went to see a weird witch doctor about my release.

'Dan,' I said, 'don't do that.'

'I just want you to come home,' she told me.

Then Daniella's friend, Page-3 model Sam Fox, who was a new Christian, invited her to church. That's how Daniella started going to Holy Trinity Brompton in Knightsbridge, where she got talking to one of the curates, Nicky Gumbel.

One Sunday, I rang Daniella. I had an unusual peace, a mellow feeling; not a druggie mellow, just an incredible peace which lasted all day. 'I feel really good today,' I told her.

'You know, Nicky Gumbel's been praying for you,' she replied.

I believed in something, but I wasn't looking for Jesus. Yet I started to get involved and attended the Bible study in the prison chapel.

It set alarm bells going for others in the nick. Everyone was going, 'What are you doing? Have you got a move in there? Is something going on?' They couldn't understand why I would be in chapel, so they thought I must up to something nefarious.

Actually at first I was really just looking for a get-out-of-jail-free card, and everything was a manipulation to benefit Michael. But then I used to process the Bible study – and I came to see it as a gift.

On the anniversary of my brother's death, Dad and I went to pray in the chapel with the prison chaplain, Bill Birdwood. Martin's death had been very traumatic and we wanted to light candles the Catholic way. I remember being at the front of the chapel; it was a very moving moment, and it helped me. But I knew I couldn't be a baby in prison.

While we were praying, I nearly fell asleep. My dad told me off after we left the chapel. He said, 'How rude of you to fall asleep while Bill was in prayer.'

I continued to medicate with drugs. If prison officers went, 'Emmett, we can smell it out here,' I'd get the talcum powder out and fire it at the bottom of my door so the smell disappeared. They knew that talcum powder was the cover-up for the cannabis, but it was harmless.

Mandatory drug-testing then came in. The prison officers said, 'Emmett, do yourself a favour and stop. If you don't, we're going to drug-test you and you could get an extra twenty-eight days added to your sentence.' They'd marked my card. I thought that I would never be able to stop. I was an addict – cocaine was my mate.

By now, Daniella had started to visit less. It was the day of the World Cup quarter-final with Italy and she was watching it with her dad, instead of being with me. I wasn't happy about it and got very childish on the phone to her. Really it was a beautiful summer's evening with the sun shining through, lighting up the floor of the wing; and I was thinking, 'Oh, this is nice.' But then we argued and the mood changed. Looking back, it was complete rubbish, but I'd had a couple of joints of skunk. I had no filter to understand the situation.

Next, I rang Tracy and we had an argument about money. She told me not to call her for a while. I exploded. Whenever I exploded, I would rant and rage for two or three minutes. People used to get a bit frightened, but I didn't do it to scare anyone; it was just me.

Then my dad shouted over the balcony, 'Shh, get in here. Don't let these people see any of this.'

'Okay,' I said. Everyone was watching me; it was pretty shameful. As I made my way upstairs, I told the other inmates, 'Get out of the way. Get out of the way.'

When I walked into the cell we still had about 15 minutes until bang-up, but my old man closed the door. He said, 'Let's sit here together.' I rolled him a little joint and he got his art out. I had these two situations whirling around in my head: one, Daniella; two, Tracy. My brain thought, *Get stoned.*

On the third joint, I had a panic attack. It frightened the life out of me, so I started counting the bricks.

'What's the matter with you?' Dad said. I'd gone white.

I jumped up at the window, from where I could see the top of the pub and hear a guy down there speaking. That pulled me back to reality, but I was really frightened. I thought, *My god, I'm losing my brain.*

I woke up in the morning thinking the panic attack would have passed, but it hadn't; the panic was still there. My dad kept on asking me what the matter was.

'Oh, I'm all right, Dad,' I said. 'Leave me today.' And I stayed there in my cell. It was overwhelming. I thought, *What am I going to do?*

During a visit from Rosheen, who by now was married to my dad, I got a chance to talk to her.

'Look, don't say nothing to Dad, but he's lied,' I told her. 'He's having trouble sleeping. Can you get me some temazepam for him? But don't let him know that's what I'm going to do. I'm just going to give him one a night.'

Rosheen was a psychiatric nurse. 'Are you sure?' she said.

I said, 'Yes, I'm positive.'

Really the temazepam was for me. Dad was sleeping like a lord; nothing bothered him. But two days later, Daniella brought the temazepam in on a visit.

No one knew it, but I was in turmoil. To get rid of the

panic, I medicated myself on that sleeping drug every day for two weeks.

Then one morning I woke up and just thought, *That's it.* I looked at the pills. *I don't want this stuff no more.*

I closed the door, put my pillow behind my back, and picked up the Bible – the Gideon's Bible, which is in every prison. In the concordance at the back, there was *depression, failed marriages*; it was all there. I looked at a number of the passages but there was one verse which stopped the noise in my head – even if only for a nanosecond. Matthew 17:20:

> *If you have faith as small as a mustard seed, you can say to this mountain, 'Move from here to there,' and it will move. Nothing will be impossible for you.*

As I read the verse, something happened. I thought, 'My god, I feel all right.' I was so happy. Even when the feeling left, it didn't take me back to the pain that I was in. Something had shifted.

I had nothing to hold onto, only bad news, and I had nothing to get high on since I was fed up with the adrenaline from arguing. I didn't like the lows so I started venturing to the chapel. 'I want you to come along,' my dad used to say. 'Just pop along every now and then.' His faith was very similar to mine; maybe that's where I acquired it. He would go and sit at the back of the church and make himself known to the chaplain.

A lot of people in prison went to chapel. Some went to do naughty things, others just to be away from the noise, because it was so bloody noisy in prison – bang, crash, the whole time.

The chapel was stone-brick, made up of two or three levels of ten cells knocked through together, with velvet drapes, high ceilings, and the Stations of the Cross on the wall. There was a big organ at the back. Along with the chaplain, Bill, there was a guy who used to help him out called John Copin, an ex-addict who struggled badly with his own demons. However, he came alive when he was helping other people. John really desired the Holy Spirit because of his own brokenness, so it was full-on, but not over-the-top. We just felt his compassion. It was as if he was saying to us, *I want you to get this, boys.*

One day, John got up at the end of a service and said, 'Those who want to believe in Christ, stand up.' There was an atmosphere in the room that prompted me to stand up. John then asked us to say the Sinner's Prayer and to take a few moments to ask God's forgiveness for anything that was on our conscience.

Lord Jesus Christ, I am sorry for the things I have done wrong in my life. Please forgive me. I now turn from everything that I know is wrong.

Thank you that you died on the cross for me, so that I could be forgiven and set free. Thank you that you offer me forgiveness and the gift of your Spirit.

I now receive that gift. Please come into my life by your Holy Spirit to be with me forever. Thank you, Lord Jesus, Amen.

I shouted the prayer at the top of my voice.
'Are you all right?' a young man asked me.
'I don't know,' I said. 'I just felt inspired to do it.'

I woke up in the morning thinking, *What have I done?* But at the same time I felt that nothing had changed: I was still Michael, who would do whatever he wanted to do.

13. BAPTISM OF FIRE

One day in my cell, I was reading the *Mail on Sunday*, which I got every week. There was a big story in the middle of the paper about Holy Trinity Brompton, known as HTB for short. Something spiritually was going on there; people's lives being turned around for the better. Everyone was showing up at HTB to see what was happening. I said to my old man, who was on the bottom bunk, 'Cor, that's the church that Daniella is going to. I'm going to go and show Bill.'

I flew down to the chapel and told Bill, 'Give Nicky Gumbel a ring, because he's been praying for me.'

'Oh, that's exciting,' said Bill and got Nicky on the phone. He had just finished a service.

After Bill had spoken to him, I asked for the phone and said, 'Hello, hello, Nicky. I've heard all about you.'

He said, 'We're praying for you. How are you?'

'Yes, I am all right. Why don't you pop down and see us in the church?' I asked, because I knew Bill used to invite some outsiders to speak in the prison chapel.

A few weeks later, Nicky sent Emmy Wilson to Exeter. She used to be a nurse, but then she'd joined the staff of HTB and become involved in prison work. It was like Mary Poppins had come down. Very posh, she looked like Princess Di, wearing a jumper with sheep on it and a white ruff underneath, then red corduroy trousers with green socks, and a little pair of brogues with a small heel. Along with Emmy, there was Lee Duckett, who was a telephone engineer and one of us, and some posh guys – Mark, Tobias, and a few others.

They were totally out of their comfort zone. Twenty of us rocked up to the chapel, including me and my dad. Most of us were hardened criminals, tough kids, who could rip your head off.

Emmy came up and she started singing a worship song. The song involved actions. Emmy was shapely, so when she bent down, many of the guys went, 'Look at them!'

I said, 'Oi, pack it up!'

Everyone was singing and it was an easy song to follow. Emmy did it again and we're all going 'deep, deep'. We were like kids now, starting to enjoy ourselves and having a bit of a giggle about who could bend the lowest. Then the song stopped and Emmy asked Tobias to pray.

There were not a lot of Christians in the room. I included myself as a Christian because I'd said the Sinner's Prayer and declared it out loud. Tobias said a very simple prayer: 'Come Holy Spirit.'

Suddenly, people began to laugh, cry and there was a real sense of spiritual healing. Everyone had an experience with the Holy Spirit – all twenty inmates, just in twenty different ways.

Emmy was looking at us all and saying, 'Ooh!'

'Emmy, look at them,' Bill cried out. 'Our Father's got his children.'

I was thinking, *Oh my god.*

The Scottish guy next door to me, John Rutherford who worked in the kitchens, got really frightened and went to leave. I said, 'Don't leave.'

He went, 'Michael, this is not right.'

'Do not leave. This is the most important moment of your life.' I don't know what made me say that, because I didn't understand what was going on.

Then the Spirit of God touched me: it was like someone blew at me; like a cloud of love went up. A tear came to my eye and I heard the word *hope*.

I sat down on the chair, and thought, *It never has to be like this any more.*

The only thing I can relate it to is the birth of my first daughter, but it was more intense. It was a feeling of beauty, and particularly freedom. I just got hit by it, speared by it. Something went on in that moment. It wasn't a figment of my imagination; it wasn't a weird out-of-body experience. In fact, it was very, very normal. So normal that it became real.

Looking back, I think the experience had a lot to do with the preparation of my heart – the verse about the mustard seed, the Bible studies, Nicky praying. I wasn't aware that I'd done it, but I'd opened myself up to be available.

The prison officers saw it too, and must have been touched. But they were getting concerned. It was off-putting. We were all over the place, not really sure what was going on. Everyone in the room felt it: a peaceful chaos; something powerful.

Then I came to and made myself busy trying to work out what was going on. Now I wanted to get to my old man. The prayer had knocked him on his back, and you couldn't knock Dad over without him getting up. I ran up to the old boy where he was on the floor laughing. As a person, he was usually a bit miserable, and I'd never seen him laugh like this. I thought he had wind or something. There was a feeling of protection in me: no one was going to embarrass or hurt him. Subconsciously, this was the criminal way, but the roles were beginning to be reversed – he used to be the protector, now I was becoming his protector. So I went to him, 'Oi, stop!'

Then abruptly it all ended. There was a time schedule and it was bang-up time.

No one wanted to leave. It had been such a moment of happiness, joy, and gladness. They were the moments you needed to steal in prisons because the comedown in prison is pretty hard.

We all headed back to the wing and I put my arm around my dad. As we left, the Senior Officer said to my old man, 'You're drunk, Emmett.'

The old man looked at the SO and said, 'When you cry, you cry alone. But when you laugh, the whole world laughs with you. But now, when I cry, I've got someone to cry with. I'm not drunk; I'm high on the Holy Spirit.'

I thought, *Where has that come from?*

'Get me home, son,' said Dad.

Everyone in the nick knew something had happened. Word went around like wildfire. They didn't expect to see me and the old man coming out of a service, since we were well thought of. Going to church was definitely seen as a weakness. It went against the grain of any criminal's thought patterns. But we walked back to our cell, went to sleep and woke up feeling great.

I went downstairs and a mate came up to me. 'Have you got any puff? They haven't got any over there.'

I had but I'd hidden it and didn't want to go near it, so I said no.

He went, 'Are you coming down to have a puff tonight?'

I said, 'No, no, I'm not.'

Life had suddenly changed for us, as it was changing for inmates around Britain. Very quickly, there was a lot of stuff going on in prisons, with people praying and Bible studies. It was really the beginning for Alpha in Prisons, an introduction to the Christian faith, which God used to reveal himself in hope. With its roots in what Nicky Gumbel had been doing at HTB, it was a non-pressured course for the broken.

During this time, I saw a lot of John Copin, the ex-addict who used to help Bill in the prison chapel. We became great buddies. He would bring in filtered coffee and Dolcelatte cheese. I loved Dolcelatte.

'I got the cheese,' he'd go. 'Have you got the biscuits? We'll have coffee today.' So we would have filtered coffee and Dolcelatte and talk about the gospel.

Other times my barrister Jonathan would visit, as our trial was now approaching. But instead of meeting me on the solicitor's visit, he would arrive late at eight o'clock at night when we were all banged up and ask to get me out. We would sit in the empty wing and chat. He would always bring me something to eat and go, 'How are you, Michael?' He would talk to me like everything was brilliant. He liked to say about my crimes, 'Great story to tell your grandchildren at Christmas, Michael.'

On 20 December 1994, after a year on remand, Dad, Peter Bracken, Dennis Lemmonier, and I were sentenced. There were armed guards outside the court. We were looking at twelve-and-a-half years and a £3-million fine. We had all pleaded guilty and tried to do a deal.

Dad said, 'I have never dealt with them. I have never given in to these people. All they want to do is bang you up.' They were the enemy. My dad was angry that his cover had been blown and that it was his son who blew it. But I was an addict, and so I was mad and irrational.

I wanted to get Dad out of it. When Jonathan came down to the holding cells, I said about my dad, 'Listen, I'll take it on the chin.' Then I asked Jonathan to do me a favour and go upstairs to speak to Garlick, the prosecutor, who had a bad stammer and always spoke very slowly.

Jonathan said, 'The only thing that would help would be to give up bodies, but I know that you and your father don't tell tales.'

I told him, 'I've got a guilty plea that'll save a fortune on a six months' trial. That's what I've got to give them.'

'I'll see what I can do.'

But when Jonathan came back from upstairs, he said, 'Listen, it's your dad they want. It isn't you, it isn't Bracken; it's your dad.' He told me, 'You'd better tell him.'

'You tell him,' I said. 'I'm not telling him that news.'

We were all in our holding cells, eating fish and chips. I said, 'Dad. Jonathan wants you.' By Dad's body language, I could see he thought it was good news. Jonathan told him through the hatch of his prison cell.

All hell broke loose. Dad's expression changed; his chest got bigger; he was fuming. He swore and started shouting at everybody in the room. He blamed me and called me greedy. But that's how it was. There are no free lunches. Dad had got caught.

He was first to be sentenced.

'Don't stand up,' Judge Neville told him. 'I am glad you are at the mercy of the courts. This is an international crime. I sentence you to twelve-and-a-half years.'

Dad erupted and attacked Lemmonier in court.

I was sentenced next and also got twelve-and-a-half years, as did Peter and Dennis. It wasn't a great Christmas present. Peter looked at me, and I sensed that he was pleased I had been sentenced; he was happy that I hadn't got out of it. But the fine of £3 million went down to £400,000, which was £100,000 each. It was a carrot so we would make a deal to plead guilty.

Mum was in court. She always conducted herself in a very, very humble way so that everyone looked upon her as the backbone. The only thing that was noisy about my mum was her laughter: you could hear her laugh in the street; the most beautiful laugh. But the noise when I was sentenced frightened me. I wasn't aware that that level of noise could come out of my mum; that volume of noise of her love was something I had never experienced in the whole of my life. It came out like 100,000 people screaming, and everyone in the court stopped.

She broke down. I had never seen her break down before in all my life. But I was her boy; she had already lost one of her boys, now the other was gone. It wasn't until they mentioned my name that she wobbled.

The four of us – me, Dad, Peter, and Dennis – returned to Exeter. While I was waiting in reception to be given my prison clothes, I looked through the crack of the door. I could see my dad and I watched as one tear came out of his eye. He was weeping for his son. Dad was hurt big time by me getting that sentence. I felt sad for him. It was certain things like that which reminded me how beautiful he was. Then he pulled himself together and came up to me like a soldier in a regiment, as if saying, *Right, let's get on with this*.

There had been a honeymoon period after the Holy Spirit chapel service but, when we got sentenced, it started to change.

On 13 February 1995 in the prison chapel, Bill married me and Daniella. Daniella looked beautiful in a blue suit. Normally, people are only allowed a few guests but I was allowed to invite thirty people; a mixture of inmates and outside guests. There was tea and cake afterwards.

By now, Sam Fox and Daniella had become good buddies. I had started raising money for disabled children, so I invited Sam down to deliver the cheques to various homes for the disabled. One of Exeter's prison officers accompanied her: Roy Debelle, a lovely guy, albeit it a bit of a weird one, who used to eat egg mayonnaise sandwiches every day. Sam's last port of call was visiting us in prison. Most of the inmates were locked away. Only my friends were out – all my codefendants, and Ian and John from the gym. Then there was Bill Birdwood, John Copin, and Roy. We were having a jolly-up with tea and cakes in the chapel. Sam looked to die for, wearing a jumpsuit tucked into thigh-high boots. She wanted to see the wing – the inmates couldn't believe it was Sam Fox. The local papers covered Sam's visit to the disabled homes and the prison, which received prestige.

Another time, I invited my mate Jimmy White, the World Snooker Championship player, to visit the prison. Jimmy used to do tournaments with Dad, and I had known him for years. Jimmy said yes and everyone was very excited. The two worn-out snooker tables on A-wing were repaired. ITV's *News at Ten* asked to come down. We sold tickets and raised about 1,500 quid for charity.

On the big day, I got a phone call from Jimmy saying he couldn't make it. Instead, he sent Ray Reardon, a big snooker star, who was known as 'Dracula'. But Ray was an ex-copper and if he'd known it was me organizing it, he wouldn't have come.

As he walked in, I said, 'Hello, Ray.' Straightaway, from the look on his face, I could see he wasn't happy.

Still, he was a professional. Ray did all the trick shots and took photographs with us all. Then he played two games, one with the amateur and one with someone from the nick. We had 280 inmates hanging over the sides watching. All the cameras were there. Everyone loved it. It was brilliant: like a wedding, a feast.

By June 1995, the authorities at Exeter wanted us out, so we were sent to Swaleside Prison, which is a Category B (second-highest level of security), on the Isle of Sheppey in Kent.

14. DOING BIRD

Swaleside was tough. Built like an American-style prison, it was a violent place with a lot going on. I knew many of the inmates so, when it came to my faith, I had to make choices.

Shortly after I arrived at Swaleside, Emmy Wilson came and we led Alpha meetings. Emmy represented a Christian woman in an attractive way. She didn't come with a nun's outfit or a tambourine. She had guts; Emmy was gung-ho. I once asked if she was ever frightened and she said, 'Not really, but I was apprehensive.'

The first course in Swaleside had ninety-nine people. It was a miracle – particularly in a prison which had 500 naughty boys and 11 Christians. Be it in the crooked world, the business world, or the spiritual world, I think there's always a time and a place for something to begin. There are always breakthroughs.

Alpha grew because this was its time. I had seen other courses in prison, but not what happened with Alpha.

It was not me doing it. It was God. I was a screwed-up addict. I didn't have the knowledge or the understanding. I was still wondering about what had happened. It had been so powerful in the chapel in Exeter, not outwardly but inwardly. *My god, this is real*, I thought. Everyone cries out to God if they're in danger, frightened, or worried: *Please, God, help.* I think that's how I was touched, and God continued to touch me, working through me as Alpha in Prisons grew.

But the self-consciousness began to take over. When the prison officer shouted time for chapel, these tough old criminals would go, 'You going to church, Michael?'

I would say to the prison officer, 'Look, not a lot of us go to chapel. Please stop announcing it.' But he would shout it louder. My feet were curling, but I went to chapel every time, and I did influence a number of other people.

Dad had always had a gentleness towards God and didn't have a problem reading the Bible before he was nicked. Dad was a man of many faces but, after he was touched by God, he would pray and proclaim Christ. It was his experience in the chapel in Exeter that convinced me God was really real. I used to enjoy hearing my dad talk about God, and we would pray together, even though the sense of dysfunction still hung heavy in the air. Dad and I didn't get close; there was a parting of the ways. However, the loyalty of love between father and son never left.

By now, Daniella was visiting less. The time she had spent seeing me in prison had knocked the life out of her. When we got married, she said to me. 'I don't want my dad to know that we got married in prison. I've married you because I want you to feel safe and I want you to know that I'm here for you. When you come home, we'll get married again, so Dad can think that we got married outside.'

I said, 'I get that. You know what? You don't want your dad to know; I don't really want Tracy to know.'

But she went, 'What? Why don't you want Tracy to know?'

It was as if the *Titanic* was going down.

'Well, she just doesn't need to know at the moment.'

I didn't realize it then, but a shift in our relationship had started. She wondered to herself why, after all the loyalty she had put in, I couldn't even tell Tracy.

I missed my children too. Swaleside was not really for them, so I wouldn't let my daughters visit. They knew where their daddy was, except they thought I was in prison for tax. Instead of visiting, they used to send in karaoke tunes of the Spice Girls.

While at Swaleside, on 5 February 1996, my sentence was reduced to nine years on appeal; and then, after spending nine months there in all, Dad and I were moved to Maidstone Prison. Maidstone was a very Victorian prison with high walls, but it was pretty cool and a lot of the prison officers were near retirement age. Every hardened London criminal you could think of went there. It was like we were all living in the council flats together. There were a lot of Indians too, some of them in there for domestics and some even for killing their wives, plus lots of heroin smugglers. They used to wear their collarless shirts – kurtas – on Saturdays and cook incredible food.

When I got to Maidstone, that good feeling of Jesus was beginning to leave me. I still really treasured my faith, but I didn't have any mentoring or the chaplain, and started to get in a state, harking back towards the world. I found it really hard, but I never let go of the mustard seed.

Dad found it hard too. He felt that finding God went

against the grain of who he was, and he struggled with what it meant to be a Christian. He had his feet in both camps. Then he went back to that old-fashioned belief of *God is God, Jesus is Jesus, but you've got to do what you've got to do.* But while he was in the nick, Dad never behaved like a tough man; he never went about it like he was a hood or ex-gangster. Instead, my old man was very humble.

Reggie Kray and I became friends in Maidstone. We were doing the cleaning together. The Kray twins always had a little bit of a smell about them: you could smell badness in them. Reggie knew Dad, and Reggie's notoriety didn't impress me. I just saw a broken man. He was well-defined and fit, but he was now 60-odd, very small, and had declined after 30 years in jail; he was deaf as a post.

Reggie's cell was like a Native-American tepee with all sorts of Cherokee things, and he never used to sleep on his bed; he slept on the floor instead. Reggie would come out in the morning, wearing a yin and yang nightgown with no pants on. His boyfriend, Bradley Allardyce, was just down from him in another cell. Sometimes inebriated, sometimes stoned, Reggie would call for him to go to the shower.

Then Reggie would get on the phone; he was always on calls with B-list celebrities. He used to get mail like a Christmas sack; two sacks a day. They stamped the ones with the money inside, so he only opened those. There were too many others to read. He'd go, 'Cor, I've got another 100 quid.' He was once given £200,000 by someone who'd won the Lottery. I would watch him scampering about his cell, his letters filling up half the room. His fan club was incredible.

One morning, Reggie came out of his cell, slightly drunk. He wore glasses which had a hearing aid attached to them. 'My Ronnie gave me these. They cost a grand,' he used to say. Reggie stumbled down the steps going, 'Down to Michael Emmett praying for me, I haven't got to wear my glasses any more. I can see. Michael, the Lord has delivered my sight.' Actually Reggie was still as blind as a bat. I wanted to put a sock in his mouth, and I hid in my cell.

At Maidstone, I used to help organize the inter-wing football every Saturday. I did it with Winston Silcott, who was in the next-door cell. I had seen his photograph in the paper and I was a bit wary of him. But when I'd met Winston, he was the loveliest guy. We had the same job in the laundry room, together with Reggie. Winston had heard of HTB and knew I was coming over from normal life to faith.

There'd be a Saturday football league and the winner would stay on. It was very competitive. One summer's day, we decided to do an over-40s' football game. I was the ref. The touchline was packed with inmates, most of them under the influence. It was a nightmare: everyone was fouling each other, people were getting knocked over. But it was a lot of fun. Even the officers were enjoying it.

It was a fixed match. Reggie was going to score the winning goal in penalties. I had rigged it just to give him some fun, and everyone enjoyed the entertainment. It worked out with level scores and Reggie taking the last penalty. Despite his little bow legs, Reggie was fit. But he was drunk and high on hooch.

'Go on, Reg, go on, Reg!' I said.

Everything went quiet.

I spoke to the kid in goal, then whispered to Reggie, 'Shoot that way. I know the fellow's diving the wrong way. It's his weak side'.

Someone shouted out, 'Do it for Ronnie, Reg!'

Reggie went, 'Ronnie, our spirits are entwined, brother.'

Everyone was watching him as he ran and kicked the ball. A five year old would have done a better job.

The ball bobbled; it seemed like an eternity for it to reach the goal. The goalkeeper was just waiting to dive.

But Reggie got that winning goal in the end. We put him up on the fellow's shoulders and all started singing, 'We are the champions, my friends!'

It was a moment, and it's those moments that make us cry. People in the houses on the other side of the prison could see a little bit and they put their lights on. The prison officers were looking. Everyone stopped on the pitch and we sang for about 10 minutes. There was camaraderie now. 'And we'll keep on fighting to the end!'

All of a sudden, Reggie began to cry. He looked at me and said, 'This is the happiest day of my life in prison. Thank you, Michael.' And he meant it.

The following day, a mate came and told me that Daniella was having an affair. My mate had said to her, 'You need to go and tell him. If not, I'll tell him.' I was always sticking up for her so he told me in the end. Everyone in the nick knew, because my mate was a villain as well. Eventually, Daniella came and told me, which broke her.

Daniella realized that she'd made a terrible mistake. She was only 24 – and her mates had been saying, 'Come on, let Mike go.' It was the hardest thing for her to let me go, so she went and had an affair. She finished with the guy quickly afterwards and seemed to regret it.

She was devastated and so was I. It reminded me of the death of Martin. Everything good I'd had, I'd now lost.

After Daniella's visit, Reggie was the first person I went to.

'You all right?' he asked.

'I don't know.'

'Come on,' he said. 'I'm going to take you over to church.'

We went over to the church and prayed for forgiveness with the vicar.

Reggie said, 'Forgive the man now.' I remember it – that was it: *forgive the man*. 'I've forgiven him,' said Reggie. 'Please forgive him.'

Reggie always had a 'God bless' to say, but I reignited his faith. He understood the Lord, the way most criminals do: that God is real, that Jesus is okay. He was quite a spiritual man. He knew, after 30 years in prison, that there must be something which goes on.

Then good old Tracy came to see me in prison. 'Look, I've heard that Daniella is seeing someone else,' she said. 'I'm here if you need me.'

We became friends again – and the children started visiting me for family days. I would always be funny and laughing with the kids and introduce them. I made sure they weren't sitting in the condemned places of the prison. There was a swimming pool and football pitch. I was blessed because I got into good prison environments that not many inmates would get into.

Aimee used to sit there and be quite quiet and stare.

When I was first sentenced, she had been traumatized by seeing on teletext that I was going away for twelve-and-a-half years. In her little mind, Aimee thought, *I'm not going to see my dad till I'm twenty-two.* Then there was Lillie, who was always Lil – either very happy or very sad about her dad being in prison. Beth was like electricity, on fire and always asking questions, 'Are they looking after you, Dad? What's the food like?'

She was at a private school and I said, 'Whatever you do, don't tell your friends at school.' But she did.

'Dad, I'm really sorry, but I told the girl that you were in prison for not paying any tax.'

I said, 'All right, Beth.'

When I moved to Blantyre Prison in Kent in 1997, I got slightly rebellious and started to change my ways a little bit. I never changed my opinion of God, nor could I put down the Bible, but pride started to take over. I was in a tough environment and outnumbered, so I started to be a bit corrupt, taking advantage of what I could.

But I still helped to run the Alpha course. This time a guy called Paul Cowley came from HTB with Emmy. He was a gym instructor; ex-army with a ponytail, jacket, and jeans, in boots. Dad was involved in Alpha too, but he had a difficult way of communicating with people. He didn't want to be a Christian man outwardly, but inwardly he wanted you to respect him.

Blantyre was a big house with a massive garden which held about 300 prisoners. There was a rhubarb patch, an aviary, and a little golf course. At Christmas, I donated all the Christmas trees to Blantyre. After school, the kids would come over and I would cook them curry. We had some fun in there. I would always be giving them treats and get my friends outside to go and buy them computers. I remember my old mate Bryn, from Arsenal, coming to visit too, with his wife Hayley. They had married just before I went inside. Hayley was tall, busty, and attractive. She looked the part. Both of them could have been on TV.

After a year in Blantyre, I was moved to my last prison, Latchmere. I was struggling with my faith. There would be Bible study in the prison chapel and people would ask me if I wanted to attend. I'd reply, 'No, not right now.'

One day, we received a message that my dad's youngest son from his first marriage, Terry, who was very similar to my father in his looks and ways, had been taken ill. The prison let me visit him in the hospital at Roehampton. I found Terry sitting outside. He'd been all muscle, without any spare weight to lose, but he'd lost a lot. He looked gone, with his big beard, but he knew it was me. I shaved him and put him to bed. Terry died within the month. My dad was devastated that he had now lost two sons.

At Latchmere, they worked to integrate us back into society. After two weeks' induction, we would do three months' community service, which could be visiting a dementia home, helping out at a charity shop, or taking kids riding in Richmond Park. Once we'd done the community job, we'd go to Job Club, which had things like working in a supermarket, restaurant, dry cleaners, or as a window cleaner. I worked on a building site. I would leave the prison at 7 a.m., then had to be back by 8 p.m.

As part of being back in society, we were allowed a town visit. I ran to HTB. I couldn't wait to see and feel it and go in there. As I walked in, Emmy, Paul, and Nicky met me in the church. I remember someone took a photograph of us. I loved it. It was a very exciting, beautiful moment for me. I was still a bit naive about my faith and thought HTB was where the Holy Spirit was, though He's everywhere.

In March 1998, it was Tracy's 40th birthday. Dad was very friendly with the guy who owned Leonardo's on King's Road, so I arranged a surprise birthday party there for Tracy on one of my days out from prison. It was a brilliant afternoon. Bryn and Hayley were there, as well as Brian Wright, the Milkman, and Tracy's brother-in-law Kevin Hanley (a guy who would end up banged up big-time for cocaine smuggling).

Shortly afterwards, I got my parole interview. It looked good doing courses in prison – such as education, self-awareness, anger management, and drug addiction – so I included my Alpha certificate. The lady civil servant said, 'You know what, Michael, you shouldn't even be going for parole.'

'Well, that's nothing to do with you,' I replied.

'You were doing twelve-and-a-half years. You're doing nine; you've had a major result.' She was referring to my appeal when my sentence had been cut, back at Swaleside.

I didn't like this woman, and I was thinking, *She can't say that!* But I knew she was the one who would have to make the suggestion to the Parole Board, so I decided to give it my all.

She got to the bottom of the pile of my papers and saw my Alpha certificate. 'Oh, what's this?' she asked.

'I don't want you to acknowledge that because you think I've become a Christian for my parole,' I replied.

'Oh no, that's okay.' She picked up the certificate and

saw that it came from HTB. She looked at me and said, 'Do you know the vicar of Holy Trinity Brompton, Sandy Millar?'

'Yes, I do'.

'Oh, Sandy is a very, very dear friend of mine at the Bar.'

I was the only one who got parole, and I should never have got it.

On 27 May 1998, I was released. I felt refreshed, normal. My beautiful children had their daddy back. But I felt like Bambi on ice. When I came home, Beth was nearly ten. The other girls were in their teens and changing boyfriends. I felt like I'd lost them. I wanted my little kids back on my knee. It broke my heart and really hurt me.

Mum used to write to me once a week when I was away. Always the same letter: 'Darling son, darling Michael, I love you and miss you.' I was her boy. She was over the moon to have me out.

Dad had the hump with me because even though I'd been the main organizer of the drop, he was still inside. In the end, all my codefendants did six years, and I did four years, six months. I couldn't believe it. *My god, I'm home.*

15. SPIRIT WILLING, FLESH WEAK

People were shocked to see me on the streets. No one could believe that I had got out so soon. Once I was home, my mates started gravitating towards me, not wanting me to be a Christian. I went back into the flower industry, linking up with my old Turkish florist friend Ralph again and reopening my Christmas-tree business.

One day, I went swimming at my local health club and bumped into my mate Bryn. I invited him to HTB and he started coming along. I was impressed by what Bryn had achieved, building a very successful supermarket business abroad. Bryn had a reputation on the streets of London that you wouldn't want to mess with him. He was a tough, tough boy.

Finding out that I had access to investment money, Bryn approached me about being part of the business. I said yes. It was a small company with three or four supermarkets in Tenerife and plans for much more.

At the same time, my mate Alan Royland approached me about a rock band called Syracruse and asked me to listen to their CD. No one really fancied their music, but I did and went to meet them. Bryn and I ended up investing in Syracruse to start recording, do gigs, and tour. As the guys in the band were young, Alan and I took care of them and loved them. I was like their shepherd. The three of them – Tom Meighan, Sergio Pizzorno, and Chris Edwards – used to hang out with me.

In between, I was very involved with HTB, doing talks and speaking in prisons. A lot of broken people were intrigued that someone like me had gone to church and become a Christian. It attracted a number of folks, particularly those in recovery from addiction. They were also attracted to me because I could spin a coin and get money. But that was just to fix my ego, my low self-worth. People thought I was an ex-prisoner with access to investment funds and that I didn't need help. But I did. I was a dysfunctional man.

The dark got darker as the light became apparent. All hell broke loose. From being touched so powerfully by the spirit of God, the dark was now consuming me. The sin didn't get worse, but it was more attractive and more powerful. Sometimes, even when I knew it was wrong, it seemed an easier choice and matched the brokenness which I felt inside. The Church thought I was equipped because I knew how to fight in the world. But I wasn't equipped.

I had everything going for me, then the wheels fell off. I walked into a trap. There was no police sting this time, but drugs caught me again.

In the summer of 1999, Tracy and I went to Pagham Beach in Bognor on the south coast, with a couple of my friends. I'd had a few beers. I looked at my mate and could see that he had cocaine around his nose. He really wanted me to use with him because he liked fun – and the two of us used to have fun.

'Have you got some coke?' I asked.

Tracy had taken some, but said to my mate, 'Whatever you do, don't give any coke to Michael; never again give that boy coke.' But I went to the toilet and had a line of cocaine. I stayed up for two days on it. I was like a lunatic.

So many people were disappointed by my relapse, because everyone was so excited for me to be home. But actually taking drugs was only part of the problem. Even if there had been no drugs, the addictive habit would have still been there. The problem was the addict within me.

Dad and I weren't seeing much of each other, though by now he was on home leave from prison. He wanted to get involved with shenanigans, but didn't have the guts to. He was a struggling Christian. Occasionally, we would do talks together at HTB, but it wasn't his gift because he was old-school. He didn't like getting up and talking about his old life.

On 19 April 2000, we went together to the funeral of Charlie Kray – brother of the Kray twins – at Bethnal Green. Everyone was there: Reggie accompanied by prison officers, Freddie Foreman, Frankie Fraser, and a very good mate of my dad's, Wilf Pine. All the gangsters were on one side. We wandered to the other side. My dad said, 'Don't stand over there, son, in case they take photographs.' They were his mates, but he wouldn't have it.

Reggie saw my dad and asked, 'Where's Michael? Ask Michael to come and see me.' I walked over. I loved Reggie. He said to me, 'Thank you, Michael. Thank you.' Those were his last words to me.

One evening, Mum rang and told me that Dad had

moved back into the house. Despite his four marriages, he had always loved my mum. With his other wives, he might have had the sex of his life, the food of his life – but the love of his life was my mother. He was similar to Samson, the old man in the Bible; he couldn't help himself when it came to women and, like most men, always thought the grass was greener. But although Dad hadn't been with my mum, he'd never really left her.

Martin's death never helped him; his crimes never helped him. Dad's dream had been busted. He knew it and lived in regret. When he'd asked to come home, Mum had said, 'Of course.'

When Dad came home, he expected it to be all right, that he would be king of the castle again. But he wasn't. Dad had been gone for twenty years, and the atmosphere in the house had changed. My sister Karen was living there now with her husband and three children. My dad had spent the first twenty years of my life protecting us, but he couldn't do that no more. His defects of character meant that he wasn't capable.

On 24 September 2000, we celebrated my mum's 70th birthday party at Chelsea Football Club. Dad picked her up and she said, 'Where are we going, Brian?'

The lights at the Football Club were off. I looked the business, wearing a velvet suit. As we were walking in, she asked, 'Where are we going, love?'

I said, 'Just a few of your brothers and your sister are here.'

'That's nice, love.'

When they opened the door, the lights went on. I had got my Aunty Veronica to trace my mum's family and they all came. We had 270 guests. Everyone was at the Football Club prior to Mum arriving. All the faces where there. There were people she hadn't seen for thirty years. All the balloons went up. I had the whole place covered in flowers, I'd organized a band and a fish fountain built with lobsters and prawns. It was a grand event, a proper shindig – incredible.

That Christmas was a great one. I always made sure Christmas was exciting. Tracy didn't want me to be at home, but she always loved me being there at Christmas. I used to give her money for presents and spoil the girls rotten. A few days before, I would take Tracy, Aimee, Lillie, and Beth to Harrods. We would have dinner there, then I'd buy them each a cashmere jumper, cashmere scarf, a pair of Gucci shoes, a lovely mac, or an overcoat. They used to love it. One day, Beth bumped into Ginger Spice, Geri Halliwell of the Spice Girls, which made her day.

Tracy was the most wonderful mother to my three darling girls. They came as a quartet. If you saw Tracy, you saw Aimee, Lillie, and Beth. The times I had been away meant that the camaraderie between the four of them was as if they were glued to each other. All of my daughters were very polite and a credit to Tracy. Aimee was a very watchful, very sensitive girl and very loyal to the core to me, Tracy, and her sisters. Lillie's character started to come through; she was similar to me. All little Beth used to do was talk to people.

We would go and get whatever we needed in Harrods, then listen to the Salvation Army band playing outside. The children would go home with their mum and wait for me to arrive on Christmas Eve. I made it my duty to get all the food, so I would go to Harrods and then, for the best meat, to Bob, the butcher in Northcote Road, Wandsworth. By the time I'd got the proper turkey, the cooked ham, the bacon, and the sausages, you couldn't even get a piece of paper in the back of my car, it was so rammed.

I'd phone Tracy, then pull up outside the girls' house in Sutton, which was all picturesque. The house was a big old Victorian corner house, the first house I'd ever bought, when I was about 24 years old. The girls did what they wanted in there; it was like their playhouse. It wasn't expensive and although there was nice stuff, there wasn't anything that they could ruin, and they were respectful anyway. It was a great place for them to grow up in. Their mates loved going there; they used to have fun with all the little nooks and crannies.

The girls would be sitting in the box window waiting for me to arrive. When they saw my car, they'd go 'He's here!' I would flick open the back of the car, which was electric, and bring out all of the food. Everyone was wondering what I had got. It was like Father Christmas had arrived. I used to walk in and they'd always have on Chris Rea's song 'Driving Home for Christmas'.

We would have a fish supper on Christmas Eve.

'You going to cook, Dad?'

I would do calamari, lobster, and John Dory, along with homemade chips and big salads. Mum and Dad would come round, then my sister Karen would arrive with her family. Everyone would leave about ten o'clock. I'd get ready and go to HTB for midnight mass before getting home about half past one, exhausted. Tracy would be in bed. We would get up on Christmas morning and it would be a jolly-up with people coming over and loads of things going on.

In the New Year, alongside Syracruse and the supermarket with Bryn, I launched a radio station. I invested my money and other people's money in it and went for the Worth FM licence with some friends of mine. The application process took about three years. During that time, we did lots of events, sponsoring Worthing Football Club and launching our licence bid at the Club, where they hosted Brighton every year pre-season. The actor Ray Winstone came along to represent us, alongside the ex-Chelsea football player Peter Osgood.

In between my businesses, I continued to work with HTB on Alpha in Prisons. I remember one year HTB hosted a Caring for Ex-Offenders Prison Conference. Winston Silcott came down. By now, he was a well-known face. Convicted in 1987 for the murder of PC Keith Blakelock in the Broadwater Farm riot, he had got out on appeal four years later and received £17,000 for wrongful conviction. Then he got £50,000 in an out-of-court settlement from the Met Police after he'd taken them to court for malicious prosecution. Blakelock's widow was distraught about all this. Winston had also been arrested for killing a different guy at a party, for which he had since served eighteen years.

The day Winston Silcott came to HTB, I was asked to come down and say hello as a friendly face. We talked and then I went to sit beside this other guy at the church. I didn't have a clue that this guy was PC Blakelock's best friend — the man who had arrested

Winston after Broadwater Farm. The guy had left the force and become a probation officer, then started going along to church.

At breakfast Jo Davis, who worked with vulnerable people at HTB, said to the probation officer, 'Have you been forgiven by God?'

'Of course I have,' he replied.

'Have you forgiven Winston Silcott?'

'I will never forgive him.'

'How can God forgive you?' Jo said.

'He killed my friend. I charged him. And he got over fifty grand.' He meant the £50,000 from the Met Police.

'He's been in prison for eighteen years for a murder, and they say he didn't murder PC Blakelock,' said Jo. 'So he didn't get off scot-free.'

I was at the back of the church. Jo came and introduced me to the probation officer. I told him, 'I found Winston a nice fellow. And if you want my opinion, I don't believe he did it.' The guy didn't like that.

But then one of the team from HTB came up to him and asked if he would go on stage with Winston. Winston and the probation officer went downstairs into the crypt and made amends.

Winston said, 'I've forgiven you', and the other guy replied, 'I've forgiven you'.

After they came back upstairs, they were both gallant enough to be interviewed by Nicky Gumbel on stage.

One day, I got a phone call from Bryn's wife Hayley. I knew Bryn and Hayley weren't getting on, and that afternoon they'd had a major fallout. I was always a good listening ear and there was the utmost trust among Bryn, Hayley, and me.

A few weeks later, I went to a funeral. I was dressed smart and arrived in a brand-new Range Rover; I seemed to be becoming something that the world had earmarked me for. But although I might have looked good and sounded good, I was still a traumatized kid inside.

Bryn called me to find out how Hayley was. She was at the funeral too, so I said, 'Don't worry, she's with me.'

When day turned to night, Hayley and I went to a nightclub, and as we were leaving, we kissed.

'No one's ever done that to Bryn before,' she said.

I went home thinking, *Oh my god.*

The following morning, I went to Hayley's mother's house to get my car. I'd left it there the day before because I was drunk. But Hayley was there, and she had left her home with Bryn. So we went out for dinner and tried to talk about things. Then the inevitable happened and we began an affair. So now devastation was just waiting around the corner over those friendships.

Shortly afterwards, I stopped taking drugs. I didn't want to be in that dark place again; the brokenness was still apparent from previous times. I started running a small church discussion group at HTB, but even though I was God-filled, I still wasn't healed. That beautiful feeling of God eluded me.

16. TWO WORLDS

A few months later, I was at my flower pitch in Wimbledon when a mate of mine under police surveillance came to see me and handed me a parcel. It was a thank-you gift from years gone by. As I received the bag, the police took a photograph. Customs and Excise were already onto my mate, but they became convinced that I was involved and mounted an operation on me. The next day, the lady who lived in the posh apartment above my pitch came downstairs and said to me, 'How bizarre. I've just come out of my house and I'm not sure, but I think there were two men taking photographs of you.'

I walked round and saw two men get on a motorbike. I knew immediately they were police.

Then, back at the flat I was renting on Tregunter Road, on the edge of Chelsea and Kensington, my French neighbour suddenly appeared and told me, 'Someone is repairing the intercom. But there is nothing wrong with it.'

By now, I was really alert. I thought that the police must have bugged it.

Then I decided to drive to see the builders working on the basement flat I owned in an old Georgian house on Onslow Square, close to South Kensington Tube Station.

A therapist mate of mine, Nick, was with me, and as I leaned over from my seat to open the passenger door for him, by a fluke I saw a guy at the nearby bus stop and realized he was a copper.

Normally I'd have told the copper to get lost – not because I was anything special; just that when they came for me, they came to nick me. But this time I just drove around the corner and pulled across the road so I had my wing mirror directly on the bus stop. The geezer didn't know that I'd seen him.

When I pulled off again, I saw the guy at the bus stop hailing a taxi. I was right. I said, 'Nick, I'm being followed by the police. But it's all right; just sit tight.'

When I started driving towards South Kensington Tube Station, the taxi went to follow me, but it was facing the other way. I stopped at the traffic lights and the taxi moved to do a U-turn to come behind me. So I did a U-turn myself. Now the taxi couldn't do another one, since it would be too obvious they were tailing me. So I parked up and waited. I didn't just want to lose him; I wanted to make sure I'd got him where I wanted him.

The taxi went off around the one-way system at South Kensington and came back to find me still there in my spot. The copper in it still didn't realize that I'd seen him. When I turned into another street near Onslow Square and parked, the taxi driver followed but couldn't find a parking space. He either had to drive off or give the game away, so he drove off. Once he'd gone, I pulled out again and drove on. I'd decided against visiting the basement flat.

By now Nick was petrified. 'It's all right,' I said. We got out of the car a few streets away from Onslow Square, about halfway back towards the Tregunter Road flat we'd come from. As I walked along with Nick, I was alert. A guy who I thought was a copper was looking through a gate at me, and as I went around the corner he came out from behind the gate. I stared at the guy over Nick's shoulder, and he walked past me. So I turned Nick around and I was now walking behind the policeman. He obviously knew where I lived, but when he walked along Tregunter Road I just carried on walking.

Nick had somewhere else to go and he left. Alone, I crept back around to my rented flat there and got into the front garden, from where I could watch the guy. Very casually, he walked down the road so I started to follow him. When he walked round the corner and into a flat in Redcliffe Gardens, I finally thought I'd mistaken him, and I went home. But then I had second thoughts. Going back to look at the building he'd gone into, I realized it looked directly over my flat. *Now, hold on a minute*, I thought. They were definitely watching me.

Later that week, I came back to my Tregunter Road flat with a drop-dead-gorgeous Danish girl. She began to get undressed, and was wearing red velvet underwear. But I thought, *Oh my god, I'm with the Lord!* I didn't want to make love or have sex. So I said, 'I'm really sorry, no, but you can stay the night.' She slept in my bed and I put the Bible between us. (Other times, I would say to girls, 'Look, I'm sorry, can we pray?' They thought I was nuts.)

At five o'clock in the morning the Danish girl woke me up and said, 'Michael, you're snoring so loud, it feels like an aeroplane is landing.' I walked into my kitchen. I had a bad back so I stretched and, as I did, a light came on in the window of the building in Redcliffe Gardens from where I believed the coppers were watching me. That confirmed they were bugging my flat.

Telling the Danish girl, 'I'm going out, won't be long,' I went to investigate. I started walking down the road and, as I turned around the corner, I saw one man. He really didn't look like he was going to work, so I walked up to him and said, 'Leave me alone; I've done my time, leave me alone.' The man didn't say a word, just walked past me.

That was it: they stopped using the flat, so I thought everything was cool. I was wrong.

A month later, I was on my way to meet a man who was known as the Con. He was the brother of a lively chap known as Chips, who had introduced himself to me at Maidstone. He knew his way around prison.

I pulled up with my builder Dave in my red Range Rover at one of my family's flower pitches, opposite an antiques shop in Chelsea. Apparently the police had asked the antiques shop owner if they could take photographs of me.

When I walked into the restaurant Bibendum, by coincidence there were two of my old associates there. Although it looked like I was meeting them, I wasn't. Suddenly someone came in and warned me that three carloads of coppers were outside. I sat talking to the Con, but when one of the coppers walked into the restaurant, I said to my mates, 'Look, I'm going to slip. You lot stay here; it's me they're here for, not you.'

Dave was still sitting in the car when I walked out to it. I recognized one of the coppers' cars; it was a big one, so this obviously wasn't a surveillance but an arrest. It made me think about what was in my glove compartment – a cheque and a watch – and how they could be taken off me just like that. They were going to pounce and arrest me there and then, I thought, but they didn't.

Rather than spark a police chase, I decided to take it slowly and make sure they could all see me as I left. I drove over Chelsea Bridge then up Queenstown Road, knowing my route and going really, really slow, sometimes doubling back. What I wanted to do was keep all three cars where they could see me; I was being a little bit clever and wanted to know where each of my pursuers was.

Meanwhile I got my two phones out of my pocket and started dismantling them. There was private stuff on my phone which I didn't want the police to see. Dave was wondering what I was up to. He was a decent and straight guy and had never been in trouble before in his life, but he knew I had a dark past.

We were now getting towards my flower pitch at Clapham South Tube Station. All three police cars were behind me and I was not going to speed up because if I did, they would go straight for me. They knew that I was going to the flower pitch and must have thought, *Right, we're going to get him here.* But the coppers didn't know that I knew they were there.

I had gone cool. Now that I'd avoided a high-speed chase, I wanted to give them the slip quietly.

Dave asked me, 'What are you doing?'

'Listen, Dave, we're being followed by twelve coppers.'

He was a ginger – naturally pale – but I could see the colour drain out of him.

'Dave,' I said, 'it's all right.'

I drove past the Clapham Common cricket green and parked. Two of the cars parked too, but one went past me. Then instead of getting out, I drove off again. The car that had gone past me turned right, so I turned left. With no police now in sight, I slowly pulled up outside the flower shop. My daughter Aimee was in there along with my book-keeper, both busy working. I parked and said, 'What I am going to do is get out of the car. You can get out of the car and do whatever you like, but just walk away, Dave, all right?'

Getting out of the car, I put my two phones down the drain. By now I could see the coppers running across Clapham Common towards me. Using an entrance that no one really knew about, I ran into the shop. I'd brought my stuff from the glove compartment and I said to Aimee, 'Put this watch and cheque down your knickers, then phone Grandad and tell him to meet me where I was born.'

I ran through the other door and jumped the Tube barrier. Trains came along every minute so I was on the Tube going to Stockwell within seconds. The coppers ran into the shop and saw the other door, but I was already gone. I was away.

My dad was there within 40 minutes. I said, 'They're onto me.' He got me out of town and we went down to Bournemouth for a few days.

Looking back, the police must have been watching me for quite a while. Next door to my Clapham Junction flower pitch was Operation Trident, the investigation unit for black-on-black crimes. They knew me and they'd been saying to me, 'You haven't changed. Your dad is a villain and so are you.' Little had I known that my shop was under surveillance.

Among the madness, there were beautiful times too, with holidays to New York, the South of France, and Spain. The children went to private schools and did ballet, tennis, played the piano, and went horse-riding. They had a lot.

But with me, it was always, 'Quick, I've got to go, I've got things to do.' In September 2002, I started travelling with Paul Cowley for Alpha and saw it go everywhere. We went to Hong Kong, Canada, Kenya, Uganda, and Korea. I saw some wonderful things. I was alive in the spirit, but it still didn't heal my brokenness and I was still involved in certain things which I knew weren't right.

One of the prisons in Hong Kong sticks in my memory. I could smell the bleach on the floor through to the gym, which might have been from routine cleaning but might have meant something worse. After the time I'd been spending with some very posh Christians, the smell woke me up to where I was.

It wasn't just the bleach. I could smell danger. There were no officers in sight, and when it's like that it only takes seconds for prisoners to play up. I thought, *Hold on a minute, there's a mistake.* I said to Paul Cowley, 'Something's wrong. There's no one here.' All of a sudden, the inmates began to arrive and a prison officer flew down the stairs in a panic – I never found out why, but now I knew I must have been right to sense danger.

We walked up the stairs to a room with no windows. About eighteen guys came in, all dressed in tunics. I was there to share with the Hong Kong equivalent of Emmy

Wilson. She was a beautiful lady, married to an English guy.

I got up to talk and said to the translator, 'Tell them they're allowed to smile.'

She said, 'I can't say that.'

It was a hard-going 20 minutes, locked in a room with no windows and no air, with the prisoners, all in grey prison uniforms, just staring at me without saying a word. It was like there was no one in the room. In the end, I turned to Paul and said, 'I just can't do this, mate. This is mad.'

'Okay, I'll come up,' Paul said, and he came up to do his bit. All he did was point at the cross. As he did, half of the men in the room started to cry. In my ignorance, I didn't realize the Holy Spirit was at work. It was powerful.

The prisoners then wanted me to pray for them. The majority had been nicked for murder and were telling us, 'It wasn't me.'

I said, 'All right, maybe not. I don't know.'

They said, 'I didn't do it. Can you pray that the judge releases me?' They didn't understand English that well, so we just prayed gently about their lives. I found it very moving.

From the prison, we went to see a British lady, Jackie Pullinger, a missionary who helped addicts withdraw from drugs through prayer. Jackie had houses where the addicts lived, separated by various levels of sobriety. Volunteers came from all over the world to do prayer-watches, praying constantly for two or three hours at a time over addicts coming off drugs.

At one of the houses was a big half-Canadian, half-Chinese guy; a seaman with deep-blue eyes, black Chinese hair, and hands on him like shovels. He had failed to come off drugs a few years before, and was now trying again, though it wasn't so much drugs now, it was drink. He came out of the house in his dirty feet, with no shoes on. Jackie's team asked me to prayer-watch him, saying, 'You have to follow him everywhere he goes and take care of him. Then you end the prayer.'

There were usually two prayer-watchers, but I was left on my own with this guy. They said, 'You've got to do it for two hours.'

God, that's a long time, I thought; so I asked, 'Can I do an hour?'

'No, you're on a prayer-watch.'

It was so quiet, no noise, you could hear a pin drop. The presence of God was tangible.

The guy came up to me and asked, 'Okay, what are you going to do if I need the toilet?'

'I don't know,' I replied.

'You want to watch me go to the toilet, man to man? They said you've got to follow me everywhere.' He kept on repeating it. This guy was about a week into detox; it was crazy.

'Okay,' the guy said next, 'what would you do if I went out that door there?'

By now, I just wanted to pray. I didn't care if it was five hours, I wanted to stop this geezer. 'Well, the security guard is out there,' I said.

But my own dark stuff was beginning to emerge; the prickling on my neck.

He kept going on and on. 'What would you do then if I tried to escape?'

'Mate . . .' I could feel myself losing it.

'What would you do if I hit you?'

Finally I forgot where I was and lost my temper. Standing up, I told him, 'I'd hit you back.' The insanity had come on. 'Now, shut your mouth and sit down.'

Volunteers rushed over, saying, 'Michael, Michael.'

I said, 'No, I'm all right,' and I calmed down.

I returned home and continued to push my bid for Worth FM. Having been one of the radio stations at Glastonbury the year before, we were on a roll. On 16 February 2003, we did all the sound at the Peace March against the Iraq War at Hyde Park, which over 750,000 people attended. During the march, we interviewed Labour MPs Glenda Jackson and Tony Benn, and the American preacher Jesse Jackson. There were a few royals and massive security, but I had a pass since I owned the radio station. *If only you knew my background*, I was thinking.

Looking at me, lots of people used to think, *He's it.* Little did they know how broken I was.

In between the radio-station work, I was getting more involved with HTB, often talking on stage about my criminal background. A celebrity Christian – that's what I was becoming, and I could see it. I didn't want to be one, but I had the gift of the gab, the car, money, the looks, and the pretty girl. My choices were often still dark but, looking back, I can see that my recovery was a process of elimination. I knew I was going against my faith so my faith started to impregnate any love, joy, peace, and happiness I was feeling. I used to look at the Old Testament and hold on to how God loved even the most broken of people.

The following year, I went to Uganda with Paul Cowley, Emmy Wilson, and a number of other HTB guys. People moan about English prisons, but you wouldn't want to do bad in that country. There were 5,000 inmates in a space only big enough for 600 people; they stood next to each other and took it in turns to sleep. The prison stank. It was heavy stuff.

Travelling on to Kenya, I joined the Christian charity Compassion, which works to get children out of poverty. We visited a school in Kibera, Kenya's largest slum and one of the worst in the world. The charity picked out a pupil to show us her home: a very tall girl with cropped hair; eight years old, although she looked older. Where she lived was just breeze blocks with a tin roof. Raw sewage flowed down the street. Outside the door was a pram made of broken coat hangers, with a broken doll inside. The chicken was as fat as a chip.

Down this alleyway, the girl pulled back a curtain. Inside lay her dying grandmother, naked, and looking like a skeleton with black skin. The girl's mother had died of AIDS, and her father, who was Nigerian, had left when she was young.

I had 500 quid in my pocket and I went to give it to her. But one of the volunteers said, 'You know what, Michael? That's about you. That's not about love; that's about guilt. If you want to help this girl, set up a standing order.' It was true. It usually is about your own guilt and how you want to feel better about yourself.

The experience really touched me, and that story never left me. I don't know what happened to the young girl; I know that her grandmother would have died. But what I found amazing in those places was how happy they were with absolutely nothing.

Returning home on a Friday, the next morning I went to help run a soup kitchen outside Westminster Cathedral. The homeless used to kip around the corner. They were mainly English – some great guys and girls. My church group would meet there about seven o'clock every Saturday morning, feed them some eggs and sausage rolls, and chocolates. We'd all give them a little bit of money each, and there was community there for a good hour and a half, two hours. I really enjoyed it and found it set me up for the weekend.

My youngest daughter, Beth, used to come with me and follow me around the church. She became a Christian after she met Jackie Pullinger, the lady in Hong Kong. Beth was a big part of my walk with God. She loved it.

That summer, I went on holiday to the South of France, where I had a beautiful house. I was throwing money about like confetti; I didn't realize that it was getting in the way of God. Mum and Dad came out and all my children, plus lots of friends; it was a proper turnout. Bryn was coming out for the last week with his daughter, Francesca. I went to pick them up from Nice airport and I could sense that he was frosty.

'I've got a message for you,' Bryn said.

'What's that, mate?' I replied, looking at him in the mirror of my car.

'Hayley wants you to phone her,' he said, and then asked, 'Why does she want you to phone her?'

I knew he was suspicious – and he was right to be, because Hayley and I had been having an affair. But Hayley also had a financial investment with me, so I said, 'It's over that investment'.

'She wants to talk to you and wants to know why you've changed your number.' Bryn stared at me.

'All right, mate,' I said, 'I'll deal with it.' But I forgot to call her.

The following morning, Bryn came to me again saying, 'Hayley's on the phone. She wants your number.'

I told him I'd give the number to her. The whole family was there and the kids were playing in the pool. I couldn't walk away so I phoned her then and there.

She picked up and went, 'You dirty–'

I said, 'Hold on a minute. I've got your money.'

'This isn't about the money. If you put the phone down, I'm going to phone Bryn and tell him everything.'

'What are you doing?' I said. 'It's all right, don't worry about it. Look, give me ten minutes.'

'No, you stay on the phone,' she told me.

I said, 'Look, phone Bryn if you want. Take care.'

I put the phone down and she called Bryn, though actually she didn't tell him anything.

In the afternoon, I phoned Hayley back and said, 'Look, please, this is madness.' I drove all the way back home from the South of France and met her.

What I didn't realize was that she had been telling people about us, including a cousin of mine. About a week later, when I went to a boxing do, this cousin was there. She came up to me and went, 'What have you done?'

I said to my cousin, 'Don't you say nothing.'

'I am not going to say anything,' she said. 'But Michael . . .'

That night, I was in bed and couldn't sleep. At three o'clock in the morning the phone rang.

It was Bryn, and I had broken his heart. 'What have you done?' he said.

'You don't know what you're talking about,' I told him.

But he just said, 'What have you done? What have you done? This is the one thing I can't allow.'

That's how I lost one of the dearest men in my life.

Everything that was good, I was sabotaging. After I stopped taking the drugs, God had opened a door and I thought, *Wow, reprieved!* But then, lo and behold, a few months later, I slipped back into familiar old ways. It didn't matter how painful it became.

There was a painter doing my front door not long afterwards. When he was painting, I went outside to put some money in the parking meter and said to him, 'I'll be back in a minute.' But just as I walked out, Bryn walked in – so quick that the painter thought it was me.

'Michael–' the painter said, and was shocked when he saw two guys standing there looking ready for a fight. Seeing the photograph of Beth in the main room brought Bryn back to his senses, and he left. He loved my daughter. But the painter was shocked by what he'd seen almost happen.

Later Nicky Gumbel came to me and asked what was going on. First I denied my affair with Hayley, then I tried to justify myself, saying Bryn wanted me to give my shares of the supermarkets in Tenerife back, which I had. I was in total denial, trying to hide from the pain and the upset that I had caused this dear man. So Nicky said, 'It isn't true then about you and Hayley?'

A week later, we went on an Alpha weekend away. The weather was calm and wet. I was sitting in my car and Nicky walked past. I said, 'Nicky, I need to see you.'

'I've been waiting for you,' he said, and took me to his room, where we sat down and he read Psalm 51.

Cleanse me with hyssop, and I will be clean; wash me,
and I will be whiter than snow.
Let me hear joy and gladness;
Let the bones You have crushed rejoice.
Hide your face from my sins and blot out all my iniquity.
Create in me a pure heart, O God, and renew a steadfast
spirit within me.

Nicky and I then prayed together and I cried my eyes out.

17. ALPHA IN PRISONS

'All you've got to do is love God,' said Sandy Millar, Vicar of Holy Trinity Brompton, when my affair with Hayley came out. During that time, HTB loved and supported me, drew me close, while I tried to get on the straight and narrow. My supermarket business with Bryn was finished, but I still had five flower pitches, the band Syracruse, my radio station, and property investments in Spain.

In autumn 2003, I went to Peru with a guy called Jimmy Rice, an ex-criminal who had become a Christian. Jimmy was writing a book about the rebel groups in the mountains. We visited Cusco and Machu Picchu and stayed in an orphanage right up high, where the war had really erupted, taking coca leaves for the altitude. I loved it. We bought Chelsea kits for all the children, many who had lost parents in that troubled time. I remember going to a wedding in one of the little villages. It was incredible, with beautiful women wearing homemade flower necklaces.

Back in Lima again, we met this lady, very English and very posh, who started talking about the Marriage Course at HTB. I was just listening, not saying much, until she said to me, 'Do you know about Alpha in Prisons?'

'Funnily enough, I know a little bit,' I said. We talked,

and it turned out she had heard of me and Dad.

'You're the father and son,' she said. 'Will you come with me tomorrow?'

The next day we arrived at Santa Monica de Chorrillos, the most dangerous women's prison in Lima. She told us to be very careful. It was a tough, tough place. A lot of the ex-prisoners were now prison staff and liked to take advantage.

We had brought some bottles of water and boxes of oranges. When I was going through security, the female guard wanted me to take my trousers off and search me. I looked at the English woman, who told me to refuse.

The guard was going, 'Pantalones, pantalones.' She didn't want to search me, she wanted to look at me. I said no. She must have seen something in my eyes, so she didn't fight me about it. 'You tell us a no? Okay,' she said, got her knife out, and started stabbing the oranges to see if there was anything in them.

Inside, there were eighteen Europeans in the jail alongside a lot of tough Peruvian women – all with skinhead haircuts, jeans, Ben Sherman shirts, and boots. The Europeans had been nicked for cocaine and the Peruvians were mainly in for killings and robberies. Whereas the male was more dominant in the men's prisons, here it was the women. Their husbands would visit – all small and gentle – and the women used to sit them on their laps and kiss them.

The prison yard was like a laundry, with women's underwear and linen blowing in the wind as far as the eye could see. The inmates came down to where I was waiting to do an introduction to Alpha, sitting on a concrete chair at one of the concrete tables that were both their visiting tables and where they ate.

Turning around, I found an inmate standing there with a skinhead haircut and black eyes, just staring at me. I could see that she had something dark in her – something that I also had in the world.

'She wants you to get off that concrete seat,' the English lady said.

'Listen,' I said. 'Tell her to go and sit over there, and I'm okay.'

I gave the woman inmate the same stare, but she never backed down and just told the Englishwoman again to tell me to move.

Again I said, 'Listen, tell her from me, no. I'm staying here. I'm doing an Alpha course.' What I should've said is, *Okay, I'm sorry*, but this was the old Michael speaking.

Then the English lady warned me, 'If you don't get off, she won't hurt you, she'll hurt us.'

So finally I said okay, and moved to the other table with the European inmates, where we shared the gospel and prayed.

Just before I left the prison, an Amerindian woman came up to me and blew in my mouth. It was horrendous, and I returned from Peru seriously ill.

Shortly after I got back, I was at the evening service at HTB, sitting on the big balcony that ran around the room, and unbeknown to me, Bryn was standing directly below me. Nicky Gumbel was preaching on forgiveness – nothing to do with either of us, because he didn't know that Bryn and I were both coming. But everyone in the church knew what had gone on, and during the whole sermon I felt like everyone was looking at me.

After the sermon, Nicky said to the congregation, 'Would anyone like to be forgiven, or would anyone like to forgive? If anyone wants to do that, stand up.'

Bryn and I stood up simultaneously. I couldn't see him; he couldn't see me. The leaders in the church couldn't believe it, because they knew we were at war.

Nicky continued, 'Anyone who wants prayer, please come forward to the front of the church.' Bryn didn't go forward straight away, but he saw me walk forward for prayer.

Paul Cowley came up and started to pray for me. As Paul put his hand on my shoulder, he told me, 'Bryn is standing behind you.'

'Is he?' I was on my guard with Bryn; I knew he wasn't going to ruin me because of how much he loved me, but I still felt vulnerable as I had caused him terrible pain. I turned around.

But Bryn told me there and then, 'I've forgiven you.'

I knew it took a man and the unction of God to be able to do that.

'I love you, mate,' I replied.

By now, my flower business was buzzing. When I had been away in Peru, my business partner Ralph had opened lots of new shops very quickly and employed all these girls. I was cautious about how quickly the business was growing so I went to one of my managers, Jo, to find out what had been going on.

One thing led to another and Jo and I ended up having

a kiss and a cuddle. Although we didn't have sex, it was still naughty and should never have happened. But that was the addict within me again.

As December approached, there was a great atmosphere at our flower pitches, with lots of people coming in for their Christmas trees. One day, a nun walked past my Clapham flower shop with a caliper on her leg. Chris was the chaplain for the Roman Catholics in Wandsworth Prison; I had seen her when I was doing Alpha talks there, but never met her. About 80 years old, she wore light blue robes and went everywhere for the cause of God in Africa.

I was outside my flower shop sweeping up, and I said to her, 'All right, love?'

'Yes, thank you.'

'Would you like some flowers?' I asked, my chin leaning on top of the big broom.

She replied, 'I'd love some, but you'll get in trouble from the boss.'

'I am the boss.'

That's how we met and we became good friends. It was that old-fashioned gangster belief in God: respect the church, respect the nuns. From then on, I'd give her flowers every week, and every year I gave her nunnery a Christmas tree, a proper grand tree, along with a huge turkey and a cooked ham. I blessed Chris with a mobility scooter. She knew all of my staff; she would talk to me and pray for me, and I loved it.

For New Year, Tracy and I decided to take the kids to New York. We weren't together, but would go on holidays, spend Christmas together, and occasionally sleep with each other. It was very dysfunctional and the way I was behaving was not my belief system, but I was very old-fashioned. This was my family: I couldn't bear to let them go; I hated it.

Things took a turn the night before we were due to fly to New York. We were at a Christmas Eve party at my mate Bill's house and I said to Tracy during the evening, 'We're always together. Why don't we honour God and get married?'

She just told me, 'You've had a few Red Bulls. Ask me in the morning.' But Lillie was violently sick all night, so when Christmas morning came, the idea of marriage wasn't even mentioned.

When we arrived in New York, I was smoking a big Cuban cigar and wearing a full-length handmade cashmere overcoat with a big velvet collar, and a mink hat. That had cost me a nice few quid. We were all dressed to the nines. Besides Tracy and the children, Mum and Dad came too, along with my nephew Charles. Mum and Dad, Tracy, and I all shared a big suite at The Plaza, which was a beautiful place. The children were just down the corridor.

New York was great. We met up with my mate Wozzle, a music man and quite a character, who had connections to all of the Italians out there – the Mafia. He took us to a restaurant down in Harlem called Patsy's, which made pies. At one time the Rat Pack – Frank Sinatra, Dean Martin, Sammy Davis Jr., and others – used to hang out in the backroom.

One evening, Tracy and I talked about marriage again and she said, 'Yes, why don't we?'

We weren't together in a real relationship, but I had money and she wanted the security, plus we were mates.

I phoned up Emmy Wilson and told her. She was over the moon.

Then a few days later, Tracy changed her mind. 'You know what?' she said. 'It's mad for us to get married. You're all right; I'm all right. We're doing it for the church and the children – and that's not the right reason, Michael.'

'Okay,' I replied. 'We won't get married.'

When I arrived back from New York, I went to have a look at another flower shop that Ralph had bought, and I found Jo working there with him. She was wearing a miniskirt and fishnet stockings, with false boobs, looking like she was going out for the night.

I had tried to formulate a friendship with her, because she was gutsy woman who I liked. But now we slept together.

At first, Jo and I together had seemed attractive. Though I knew it wasn't right and that it had to end, it started to become fun. Soon, however, she fell for me and before I knew it, our relationship completely overtook my life – not the seeing her itself, but the energy that it created. The addiction kicked in and manifested itself. Our relationship got very unclean and we hit that rotten apple very quickly. I thought, *What have I done?*

She used to see me cry over what we were doing. Instead of understanding, she would take it personally. It was insane what we'd done. I was man enough to say no, but I never did. We used to have sex, then I'd ask her to pray afterwards. She thought I was mad. Jo was attractive, with a body to die for; but like me, she had issues in relationships. In the end ours got quite volatile.

About six months later, Tracy and I discussed again if we should get married. She and I still weren't having a love affair but I said yes, thinking that maybe God would bless it.

I went to Jo and said, 'Listen, Jo. I'm getting married and, as much as we've had a little bit of fun, it's against my faith. Jo, this is over, mate, please.'

She was surprised. 'That's a bit weird,' she said. 'One moment, you're getting married, then you're not. Surely you don't want to get married?'

But Tracy and I married at Chelsea Town Hall on 14 May 2004, and Paul Cowley then gave us a blessing at HTB.

A friend lent us a Bentley for Tracy to arrive at church in. The flowers were incredible and the church was full up with 250 people. My nephew Charles was the best man at my wedding; Charlie Mackesy and Paul Cowley's wife Amanda did the prayers. Then we had our reception in the Conrad Hotel at Chelsea Harbour. We had opera singers, the best DJ in London, and a Diana Ross tribute band. Christians, gangsters, villains, addicts, family . . . It was a ball, it was brilliant.

But the marriage was that yin and yang again. From the outside, everything looked beautiful, but inside the brokenness remained.

On our honeymoon in Positano on the Amalfi Coast in Italy, I looked across at Tracy and thought, *What are we doing here?* Later she told me that she had done the same and that she felt the wedding was really a celebration of the official end of our life together.

We came home to our house in Surrey and parted.

She said, 'Love, you go back to your flat, I'll go back to the house.' I said okay and went to live in my Chelsea flat.

I believe that if we'd have stuck with God throughout – if we'd taken it seriously, both been mentored, and had Christians around us – then things might have been different. But we agreed subconsciously that it wasn't a marriage. It makes me sad that the memories aren't beautiful and that it was tarnished again. I was a mixture of the good and the bad, which I had been throughout my life. I was someone with this big life, but I was always very broken in it.

Once me and Tracy had made the decision to part, I began to see Jo again. My fourth daughter Ruby came out of that relationship.

One Sunday morning, I was at the car park of the private school next to my flower shop. I used the car park at the weekends to load trees for another business I ran, which sold about 3,000 Christmas trees annually; the school was fine about it. Now I was setting up my Christmas-tree pitch, and we were all standing there, including the ten or so guys who were working for me. A Pentecostal preacher walked past and I said good morning. Her name was Sister Kate.

After saying hello and asking my health, she said, 'Are you a believer?'

'Yes, I am.'

She said, 'Why are you working on a Sunday then?'

So I asked if she fancied a cup of tea, and took her to the café across from the flower shop.

There Sister Kate pointed at Jo and said, 'See that girl there? I feel God saying you need to be careful with her.'

But I said, 'There's a child.'

'Well, I didn't know that,' she replied, 'but I still feel you should keep away from her'

I thought, *Oh, I can't do that. I don't even know this Sister Kate.*

But by Christmas I had left Tracy and stopped seeing Jo.

Jo's dad came to me and said, 'I know this situation is difficult for you. I am not blaming it all on you. It takes two to tango.' And he went on, 'I will take care of the child.'

I said, 'Well, I will as well – and thank you.'

One day Mum told me, 'Your dad's not well, Mike. He ain't right.' This was shortly before my marriage to Tracy. Mum knew my old man better than anyone. The illness continued to progress and then Dad had a stroke. The doctor who examined him could tell that Dad had actually had a stroke previously, a long, long time ago; the doctor was astounded that he hadn't felt it.

Dad never felt any physical pain but he was like a baby with emotional pain; he was a tough old git, but as weak as a kitten too – I never knew what was going to turn up. He could be the most angelic man, and I truly believe that it was only some imaginary idea of what he should be like that prevented him from excelling and being something very special.

18. DOWNWARD SPIRAL

God was starting to dismantle me. He was going, *You need to stop.* But I didn't listen.

It began in 2005 in New York. I got involved with my godson, Simon Eddy, who used to work for me. He was 21 years old, only a young kid. Simon came to me and asked me to invest in a TV production company out in New York. He told me I would get an $800,000 return. In anticipation of that, I borrowed a large amount at high interest from friends, as well as remortgaging my mum's home and my own flat in Chelsea. I then invested this money in property out in Spain.

We had an office on Park Avenue with three employees and were enjoying the buzz of New York. We had meetings with big broadcast stations, then started filming on the streets of New York, where the police stopped traffic for us. Though we thought we'd arrived, we were also a bit naive. But it was the investment money that was keeping the firm afloat and paying New York City State to get all the filming licences.

There was also a musical. We met with the star, she signed a contract, and we started paying her wages. I got my friends to invest more money. Then another contract came through for $1.4 million.

Tracy asked if I was sure, and I said yes. Dad came out to New York with my mum and came back warning me about Simon. 'He's having you over, son,' Dad said, but I replied that he wasn't.

My kids went out there and said, 'Dad, he's just mad.'

I told them too, that Simon was all right. 'Listen, I've seen the contracts,' I said.

I had too, but I met up with Simon in a hotel room to double-check.

I said, 'You haven't had me over, have you? Simon, don't do this to me. It's not the money that you've had, which is substantial; but I've gone and bought property based on what that contract should pay out to me.'

'No, I wouldn't do that to you,' he told me. But I didn't like the look in his eyes.

I decided to investigate. I had two choices: 1. one, seek help through my dad; or 2. phone up a friend who had done extremely well in America with business and knew the best lawyers in town. I phoned the friend, who sent me over to see one of the lawyers.

I showed him the contracts: the one for $800,000 and the other for $1.4 million, both signed by a lawyer. He said, 'I know that lawyer.'

So did I. I said. 'My office is next to his.'

'Be careful; this is dangerous,' he warned. 'How much money have you given him?'

I told him and he cautioned me, 'Don't give him no more.' Then he added, 'If you want me to work for you, this is what I cost.' His prices were astronomical, but he told me to go and find out whether the contracts were authentic or not.

When I left the office, I started ringing round trying to find Simon. I thought back and realized that he had been saying some bizarre things: that he was friends with Ozzy Osbourne and his wife; that he knew someone very high up in the government.

Then Simon got a guy called John to call me, saying he worked for 20th Century Fox. John faxed me over a contract for another TV programme and said, 'We need money.'

I said, 'Okay, leave it with me,' but by now I realized Simon was doing wrong. I left it a few hours then called him.

'Simon, where are you?'

'We're in LA. We're meeting some people at Fox and doing some filming out here.'

I said, 'Oh, give us your phone number.' He was staying in a motel.

I put the phone down and rang him back immediately to ask one more question. As soon as I rang the number; instead of Simon picking it up, it was John, the man who was supposedly from Fox. He didn't say his name but I recognized his voice.

I asked him straight out, 'Is that you, John?'

'No, no, no,' he insisted. 'Hold on a minute.'

This is bad, I thought, and I said to him, 'John, you spoke to me last night. You work for Fox, don't you?'

'Oh no.'

Then Simon came on the phone.

I said, 'Simon—'

'No, you've got it wrong,' he said.

'What's he doing in your room?' I asked.

Though none of us knew, Simon was gay and this guy John was actually his boyfriend.

Meanwhile our secretary from the office sent me a begging letter. 'Simon took me away from my career in LA,' she wrote. 'He took me to New York, he put me in a flat, and you were the loveliest people. What's happened? Where's my wages?'

Simon wasn't a criminal; he was just living in a fantasy.

I went back to the UK to take the children to Marbella for their summer holiday. We stayed in a big house in the hills which a friend of mine was selling. With two wings, an in-house chef, and a gardener, it was beautiful.

The children and I had a great time. They used to sneak out late at night and try to get back into the house without me knowing. One night, the guy who lived there locked all the gates. At about four o'clock in the morning I heard a noise and looked outside to see my kids all trying to climb over this gate. They all got grounded.

By now, they had realized that their dad, the king, wasn't the king. He was a dysfunctional human being. They never agreed with what I was about, yet there was so much love between us.

I arrived back in New York on the red-eye flight and was picked up by Simon's business partner Sam, an Englishman whose father worked for the BBC (Simon always talked about what good media connections he had). Knowing that Sam had always wanted to live in America, Simon had created a job for him. Sam had sold his house in New Malden, moved with his wife and two children to New York, and started working in our office every day.

But by now, like me, Sam had realized things really weren't right. I could register it from his eyes as he picked me up at the airport. But I was keeping him calm as I wasn't 100 per cent sure about him.

I asked him what was going on, but he just replied, 'I'm not sure.'

Within days, I did an abrupt turnaround and went back to England, collected my accountant from there, and took him out to New York. I was thinking, *I've got to make this official*. Going into the bank where my investment money had been deposited, I spoke to a woman there who Simon had befriended. What had Simon done? I asked. In her opinion, he had done nothing wrong; she said he had told her that he had testicular cancer. This was supposed to be why he was never available when someone needed him.

As I walked through her door with the accountant, Simon phoned in. She said, 'Oh, Michael's here.' He put the phone down straight away.

This confirmed my suspicions even more, but she just said to me, 'You're a bully.'

'No, I'm not,' I replied. 'Listen, he's had a large investment from me, and the money that remains in the bank, we have to get it back.'

I then went back to see my solicitor, who introduced me to an ex-FBI guy called Bill. I gave Bill some details and, by checking ATM withdrawals, Bill found that Simon was living deep in the gay district in Washington DC. This confirmed Simon's sexuality and that he had a boyfriend. Meanwhile Sam told me that Simon was returning to New York the next day.

After being unable to verify the contracts, the situation

with John, and the disappearance of Simon, I realized that Simon was living in a fantasy and didn't actually own this production company in NYC. My accountant and I went to Penn Street Station and met with Sam. He knew that I knew what had happened. There was a big orange bin, so I grabbed this little guy Sam by his arms, opened the bin, lifted him up, and stuck him in it. He was so small, all you could see was his face over the edge.

The accountant told me, 'Michael, stop this. I can't watch this. I'll lose my job.'

'Well, look away,' I replied. 'Go around the corner, because he ain't getting out of this bin.'

I said to Sam, 'I've got the lid. Do you want me to?'

'No, Michael. No, no, no. Come and stay with us in New Jersey and we'll get Simon.'

My accountant went home and I left for New Jersey. Sam put me in a motel. I was told that Simon was arriving the following day so I hung about. The next day, I was told that Simon had got off the train and two cops had grabbed him and taken him to the police station. I later found out that the arrest had been staged, but right then it was the worst thing to tell me. I decided that I had to get out of there.

I went back to New York and told the bank manager, 'I need a banker's draft for the remaining money.'

'You can't have it until I get clearance from head office,' she told me. Time was ticking as I knew Simon was finding ways to get the money out himself. But by now the bank manager had softened towards me. With the build-up of events, she had started to realize that it was Simon who was at fault rather than me. His cancer story, and the fact that she hadn't heard from him, had made her smell a rat too.

I was desperate to get this money as it belonged to an investor of mine. To quicken the process, I used the name of Bill, the private investigator, and pretended he was outside, standing beside the McDonald's opposite. I pointed over to a group of people and waved. I thought this pressure would make the bank manager move faster and try to bypass head office. It was a shot in the dark, but I just wanted my money back. I knew I was in dangerous territory.

My plan was working. By now, the bank manager wanted the problem off her desk. She had done nothing wrong, but whatever Simon had done was obviously seriously worrying her as well, and I could sense she was anxious to get rid of me. Eventually, after some toing and froing, I secured the funds.

Sitting at JFK airport later, I said to myself, 'New York has gobbled me up. Lord, please get me out of here safely.' I walked towards Customs and off I went.

I thought God's grace would allow me to get through all these difficulties. But looking back, I think there was so much sin in my life and so much brokenness that God knew that everything I was doing was only preventing Him coming in to take my pain and heal me completely.

I was sitting in the coffee shop opposite my flower pitch in Clapham when this Indian guy called Shakil walked in. I could see that he was a bit unsteady on his feet.

'Here's a poem for you.' He passed me it.

'That's very kind of you,' I said, starting to read it. Then I looked at him and asked quietly, 'Are you all right?'

He said, 'Why?'

'Well, I just can sense that you're not.'

'Please don't tell anyone,' he said, 'but I'm a schizophrenic.'

I said, 'That's okay, sit down.' I expected some behaviour like Uncle Johnny's, but I never saw it. He was the sanest madman I'd ever met in my life, and an intelligent man beyond belief.

He'd got an incredible story. A Muslim, he had been diagnosed with schizophrenia at the age of 14. They say he had an IQ of brilliance. He wound up in a mental home, but after he came out his brother told him, 'Do not let this be your identity', so he went back to university. He became one of my top five best friends.

Meanwhile Uncle Johnny was still the same, surrounded by books on Satanism and talking about the voice of a black woman who he thought was God. I would visit regularly. I sat on my uncle's bed and said to him, 'Do you want to say a prayer with me?'

He said he did. With me beside him, he repented about the books and his belief in the dark stuff. Johnny gave his life to Jesus.

I said, 'Welcome to the family.'

'Nanny's been praying for me for years.'

'Yes, but you've done it yourself now.'

My family used to spend a lot of great times at the football. I had seats at Chelsea and the children would come. They were real bonding sessions. I was in business with a guy who had a corporate box which we used to frequent. We would have lunch there. It was all a little bit upmarket, but very good. Other times, the band Syracruse, now called 'Kasabian' and enjoying success, would invite me to gigs. They were lovely kids. I remember going backstage at the V Festival with my children.

My teenage nephew Charles, Martin's son, always came too. I took him everywhere with me. I loved him dearly. He was a beautiful, incredible boy, who spoke very nicely. Whenever I saw Charles, I would bombard him with stories about Martin. But the flipside of the coin was that Martin wasn't spoken about at Charles's home. It used to upset me. However, I started to realize that it was right. Everyone works through their own emotions in different ways.

By now Helen had three other children with Robbie. She and he used to get upset that I showed favouritism to Charles. They asked me to stop. In hindsight, they were right. There was a little bit of hardship between me and Robbie but, in the end, it all turned out so lovely.

Also by now, Syracruse was no longer actually working with me. Not long after my honeymoon with Tracy, a record company had approached them and worked on the boys, who took off. That's when they'd changed their name to Kasabian, the name that became famous. I was now out of the picture.

My radio station closed in 2006 when we lost the bid for Worth FM. I always had a nagging feeling that we weren't going to make it. Everything around me was always big or disastrous.

I still had my property portfolio in Spain. They were very expensive, exclusive homes: some townhouses, others detached, and a couple of real beauties.

A year later, Bryn came back into my life. I was in church on a Sunday morning. It was time for the Peace, when everyone shakes hands with people nearby and says, 'Peace be with you'. I didn't know that Bryn, who had now remarried, was standing behind me with his second son, only two or three months old, in his arms. As I turned around, he said, 'Peace be with you, Michael'. Bryn passed me his child to hold and I started to weep.

19. FALL FROM GRACE

As one card fell, everything fell. The recession came. My properties in Spain dropped like the *Titanic* and devalued by 50 per cent. On top of that, I had the New York con, my radio station folding, and Kasabian gone.

I started to run to Jo a lot as I found her house a bit like a hideout. Our daughter Ruby and I became really good friends. We used to have a thing where I would make up this story that she had magic boots that she used to fly into space. What used to propel her energy was the farts from her dog. We would catch the farts from the dog, wrap them up, and put them inside her boots. The farts used to make her fly. She had a friend who was a giant, and they used to go around helping with disasters around the world, in the sky, in the sea. She loved it.

My older children were angry with me but lovely to Ruby. What had upset Aimee, Lillie and Beth was that the three of them were a unit, a very special unit. I had shifted the parameters of the family.

But the parameters would soon be shifting in other directions too, thanks to those first three daughters of mine. On 22 November 2007, Beth gave birth to my first grandchild, Paddy. He was born under a bit of stress and they had to put him in an incubator for a day, but he was the most beautiful baby.

The same day, my old associates, the Con and Chips, came to me with a business idea of buying Nintendo Wii consoles in China. I got together a big sum of money and invested it with them.

It was only a few days later that I discovered the Con had misused all my money. I was left in turmoil. Normally I might be able to pay all or some of my investors back but, instead of going to tell everybody what he'd done, I let my pride get in the way. I said, 'Leave it to me. I'll deal with it.' I then went and borrowed the money from moneylenders, landing myself with the debt. I expected the brothers to pay me, but they never did.

I lost everything. Things went really bad. There was no money left and overnight I went hugely into debt. I had to sell everything. Successful I may have seemed, but the darkness was always there and eventually it had overwhelmed me.

It wasn't because God was punishing me. He wanted me and he was trying to reach me. I think in the flesh, God slaughtered me but only because in the spirit it did me good. God gives us enough rope to hang ourselves and we learn through the pain.

I panicked. I was robbing Peter to pay Paul. I had this thing about me that I'd always get out of trouble. So, instead of surrendering the debt to God, I went and borrowed the money at astronomical interest and managed to pay 60 per cent of the debt. An incredible man from HTB called Hong gave me a substantial amount of money to help me on my way. I had friends come around my house trying to help me, loaning me huge amounts of money.

I became a prolific liar. I was so frightened. People were pressing me to find out the truth. One day someone attacked me on the street. It was hairy. But, looking back at what the Con did to me, which caused everyone so much heartache and pain, I do believe that God was in it and had willed these acts. I knew the loss of everything was right. I'd got too far in it. God had watched me borrow all this money and now he was saying 'Stop!'

The glamour of life with money, the drama of my affairs, and the ability to indulge my children had made it easy to live with doing my criminal stuff. They had distracted me from the reality of what I was up to. But the mask that I had worn was totally exposed through this debt. The information filtered out everywhere – to my family, friends, and church. It became a big story.

One mate phoned me about some money I owed him. This was another friendship I was losing, and the shame and embarrassment was coming out. Instead of 'Hello, Michael,' he just said, 'You got my money?'

I paused.

He said, 'Listen, if you don't answer me properly, I am going to tell you now to keep the money.' That meant I was in trouble.

I went, 'Hold up a minute.'

He replied, 'No, Michael. Have you got my money?'

I had two phones – work and personal – and right at this moment my other phone rang. It was Paul Cowley from HTB.

My mate on the first line was telling me to hurry up, but

Paul said, 'I've got your Charlie Mackesy paintings sold.' I had about five big paintings by the artist Charlie Mackesy; I didn't even know Paul had been trying to sell them.

'How much for?' I asked. It turned out to be the exact amount of money that I owed my mate on the other line.

After I'd hung up with Paul, I returned to the other phone and told my mate, 'I've got your money.'

He said, 'What?'

'I've got your money.' I told him he could have it tomorrow.

Phoning Paul Cowley back, I told him I needed that money urgently. Paul told me to go and see the buyer, a man from HTB, the next day.

I went to the man's Threadneedle Street office. It was full of Christians who all knew me, but I was desperate and wasn't looking at anybody. The buyer said that the paintings had been delivered and passed me a cheque. I said, 'I can't take a cheque. I need it in cash.'

He was taken aback, but he went ahead and phoned up the bank, and within an hour he had the cash for me.

I never saw my mate again after I had handed the cash over to him. But I do know that God organized that phone call from Paul about the Charlie Mackesy paintings.

When Jo started to see that I was no value to her, she gained power in my weakness and started to reject me. 'At this time,' she told me, 'moving away from you is the right thing for you, me, and both our families. And you'll be happy I did this.'

In fact, the rejection totally disturbed me. My thinking became delusional again and for a moment I believed I was in love with Jo. But the reality was I had nowhere to go. Jo was a fantastic friend to me and I loved her in my own way.

One day, I was walking in Loughton near Epping Forest, Essex, and I saw her with Ruby and some of their friends having coffee. I hadn't spoken to Jo for a while, because all I had started to do was to shout at her and be confrontational. Now I just wanted to say hello, but it didn't go that smoothly. Jo exaggerated the confrontation, using it to cause trouble for me. The police were called to what was described as 'a disturbance'. I just moved away quietly and made my way to Victoria Station to catch a train home.

While I was at Victoria Station, I phoned my sister Karen and explained what had happened. As much as we'd had our ups and downs, Karen was always as loyal as the day is long. I was devastated, vulnerable, weak, and felt worthless about the whole situation in my life concerning my family, my friendships, and the collapse of all my businesses. I was at rock bottom.

Later I was sitting watching the TV and a police car pulled up outside my house. It was over the allegations that I had caused a disturbance in Loughton. I was taken to the police station, where an officer said to me, 'This is all rubbish, mate. I was sitting next to you at Victoria Station and heard every word you said. I didn't realize it was you I was picking up.' It was incredible. I couldn't believe that this copper had been sitting right next to me when I was talking to Karen on the phone at Victoria Station about the situation with Jo.

During this time, I acknowledged Ruby as my daughter. I just thought it was the right thing to do. She was three years old.

I remember Jo saying to me one day, 'It's really funny with Ruby. She's the sweetest girl and everyone's getting on with her. Then, all of a sudden, she switches on everyone.'

I thought, *She's my daughter. You might have got rid of me, but trust me, she's sitting right in your midst.* It made me laugh.

By now, the children had had enough. Tracy had gone and I was left in the only house that remained, which was falling apart around me. I owed money everywhere. I was in a terrible state. One morning, I just prayed about Jo. 'Lord, please speak to me. Help me let this situation go away. Please, today, I want this to end. I don't want it any more in my head.'

That afternoon, I was going to meet a mate so I got on the train to Victoria; but I arrived to find the Tubes weren't running from there. I went to get a cab. All of a sudden, by coincidence, Jo's father, a cab driver, pulled up as my ride. In his taxi I could see a photograph of my daughter Ruby, who I hadn't seen for a while.

I got in, but I was embarrassed because one day I had got a bit volatile and had gone over to the house making noises.

'You warned me,' I told Jo's dad. 'I'm sorry. You've got my word that you won't hear another thing out of me.'

But I also told him, 'You've also got my word that one day I'll be back, because Ruby is my daughter. And you did promise me you'd take care of her. It's your time; I won't come near you.' He had nothing to worry about, I added, because Jo was now with another man. Finally I took out the forty quid I had in my pocket and said, 'Give that to Ruby.'

Meanwhile, Dad had started to deteriorate further. Mum said to me, 'He's not well.' He had become very bitter in his old age. Old age and bitterness do not go hand in glove. You're meant to grow old gracefully.

Dad continued to get very unwell, and was phoning up his friends asking them to give him a tenner. They were calling my mum saying, 'What's happened?'

She said, 'I've been telling you for a number of years. He's not well.'

But Dad was still well enough to understand that I had lost all of my money. He was devastated but there was also some satisfaction in there as well, because it had weakened me. His mind and heart both wanted to help me, yet he couldn't muster them with that sinister spirit within him.

One day, I was in my flower shop in Clapham. 'September Blue' by Chris Rea came on the radio. It always reminded me of Martin. The words were unbelievable. I started to sing it, then began welling up, which I hadn't done for ages. I walked out to Clapham Common and sat on the grass. In my mind's eye, I invited Martin to sit down. I said, 'I want a chat with you, Mart.' Then I said what I needed to say.

I apologized and he spoke back to my soul, saying something like, 'Thank you. I can go now.' It felt like that. I cried and sobbed and said goodbye to him. I then stood up and shook his hand, saying, 'I love you. You're free to go. I'm sorry if I've held you here for far longer than you needed to be here.'

Soon after this, I sold off the last of my five flower pitches. My eldest daughter Aimee, a very shrewd businesswoman, bought the Clapham shop. And by the time God had finished dismantling my life, I couldn't even afford a London Oyster travelcard. I had nothing. I was slung into a corner where God said, 'This is where I want you.' It was such a fall from grace. I was so ashamed that for several years, I stopped attending HTB or working for Alpha. The only thing God never took was the love of my children and grandchildren.

Including Paddy, born back in 2007, there were three grandchildren by the end of 2010. On 3 March Aimee had had my beautiful first granddaughter, Nancy. On 25 July, Beth had given birth to her second child, Gracie, little sister to Paddy. I called her 'Gypsy Rose'. From the moment Gracie appeared, she was a knockout. They were such a joy in between the troubles.

Looking back at that year, it seems like a lot of it was about birth. In 2010, I moved in with Aunty Veronica in a flat on Stockwell Gardens Estate, opposite to where I was born. I was being born again.

20. THE PRINCE AND THE PAUPER

Mum was devastated about what had happened to me. She had thought I was set up for life and that I would behave myself. But, finally after so many disappointments from me, she said, 'Son, stop. Stop.'

Amid the drama of losing everything, Nicky Gumbel at HTB asked me to meet the Prince of Wales. So, on 12 February 2010, I went to St Mellitus College, a Bible college run in partnership with HTB. Everything the church was involved in was there: the homeless, prisoners, single mothers, the butcher, the baker and the candlestick-maker. They were all in different groups. It was heaving.

Nicky brought over Prince Charles. I was just standing there, knowing I had to bow or be very polite but not remembering exactly what to do. So as Prince Charles walked towards me, I just went to him, 'All right, Charlie?' and shook his hand. Everyone looked.

Before I met Prince Charles, I didn't like him because I had a resentment towards him over Lady Di – over Diana, Princess of Wales. I couldn't help myself; I just thought he was a pompous prat. But it was all shot down in flames as soon as I made eye contact with him. I thought he was a beautiful, beautiful man.

I said, 'Next time you see your mum, do me a favour, Charlie. Will you tell her how uncomfortable those mattresses are in prison?' The prince burst out laughing. He stared at me like he couldn't believe it. All his aides around him were thinking, *Who is this guy?*

Prince Charles said, 'Of course I will, Michael'. Then he mentioned Reggie Kray and asked me about my time in prison.

'I was next to Reggie in prison,' I said. Then I started talking about the Great Train Robbery, since many of the robbers were my dad's mates.

Prince Charles said, 'I remember watching the Great Train Robbery on the news with Mother and Father. I thought to myself, *How exciting.*

Through the Marquess of Reading, another Christian, I was introduced to another royal. In his personal style he acted very royal indeed and, to me, he projected what I had thought Prince Charles would be like.

I walked up to him. First of all, he was quite regimental, then said, 'You're the fellow who asked Charles to do him a favour.'

'Charlie?' I said, and he laughed.

Then I said, 'Do you know Jesus?'

He said, 'What?'

'Do you know Jesus?'

Everyone looked at me. The royal moved on.

Shortly afterwards, I met a woman who started praying for me. She said, 'What does the name John mean to you?'

I replied, 'It means a lot to me.' It was the name of my grandfather and my schizophrenic uncle, as well as my middle name. But I didn't want to say any more; I wanted to test her.

She prayed again.

'This name has been worrying you for a while, hasn't it?' she said. 'But God's come to break that fear around the name.'

I looked at her.

She continued, 'John's not a curse, it's a blessing.' She could've knocked me over with a feather. I went up to see Uncle Johnny four days later. For so many years I had carried the fear that I had mental-health issues. It was gone. I was free.

The following year, Uncle Johnny died. I was happy when the news came through. I spoke at his funeral and went to see him in the Chapel of Rest in Epsom. There was nothing of him. He was such a handsome boy. I looked at his hands and all the rings on his fingers and his big beard. He was 78 years old, at peace for the first time, after 60 years in a mental institution. I prayed over his body. I said, 'You can have him now if you want, schizophrenia. Do what you want with him. He ain't here no more.'

In July 2012, I went to Focus, HTB's week away at Golden Sands, Mablethorpe, Lincolnshire. I drove down with Aunty Veronica, in a van with broken windows that you couldn't roll down, and air-conditioning stuck on hot. I was in trouble and looked terrible, with a tooth missing. I was at Focus to do a talk on restoration with God. Unbeknown to me, Bryn was going to Focus too. He arrived with his family in a brand-new Porsche and was staying in a caravan directly in front of my own tent pitch.

I still didn't know that Bryn was there when this little boy walked around the corner one day as I was sitting outside my caravan. He was about six but I thought, 'My god, that kid doesn't half look like Bryn.' I called him over and asked if he was Bryn's son.

'I know your dad,' I said. 'He used to have a nickname: Dusty Bin (Bryn).' It was a real emotional moment to meet Bryn's child. I had an overwhelming feeling of love for this kid, yet I didn't know him, but he looked the double of his father.

The little boy went over to his dad. 'There's a fellow over there. He said you were rubbish dust.' That didn't help.

Bryn invited me to a barbecue. Beforehand, we met in this little place. Bryn had sunglasses on so I couldn't see his eyes, but I sensed that he was very, very sad and still so hurt about what I had done to him with Hayley. He said, 'Listen to me. I loved you; I miss you. I'm sorry, mate. You helped bring me up. You helped us all – me, Tracy, Daniella – you helped everybody. I'm always in your debt but, Mike, you took something that weren't yours.'

I wept. He prayed and left.

The next day, I saw Bryn on the beach. At first it was obvious that he'd gone from the loving, kind man of the day before to hatred. But then he softened.

He said to me, 'What happened? Why have you had such a tough time?'

I replied, 'Listen, mate, I feel it was God. You reap what you sow. The journey is different for what I've done, and maybe this is my lot. Don't worry.'

'But you're so cool about what's happened to you.'

'I'm not,' I told him. 'But I do know that we're all going to be all right.'

At the end of 2012 Kim, the daughter of Dad's old partner Arthur Suttie, came back into my life. She phoned me and asked if I would like to look after her farm for a couple of months, and I said yes. I needed to hide out. I was being hounded by undesirable people about the money which had been lost.

The farm had a big house, Edolphs House, which was 400 years old. It was beautiful but falling down and needed work done on it. There were eight bedrooms, four bathrooms, a snuggery, dining room and lounge, and two inglenook fireplaces. There were bats everywhere. It was quite bizarre.

After six months, Dad came and joined me. My mum said we had to get him down there. He still had a cheeky chappy thing about him, but mentally he was gone. However, he was still that protective father and it made me feel safe having him in the house. We took in an abandoned dog and nursed her back to health. She was a Rottweiler, but so skinny that she looked like a greyhound and we called her Meg. Then we had Bert, a cross between a shitzu and King Charles spaniel, who was very intelligent. So, it was me, my dad and two dogs. A mate's son who was heavy on drugs was slung down there with us as well. He was very posh and worked on the farm.

I had quite a bit of fun. One of the dogs would chase all the sheep and nearly get shot by the farmer, who I then had an argument with. We spent our days mucking out pigs, working for nothing. The pigs were smelly but clean, using the same place as their loo every day. I was also involved in breeding and birthing the pigs.

The farm used to have one of the biggest piggeries in London, with 6,000 pigs, but there were only 400 left. I created a butcher's round. I'd get the pigs, go to the slaughterhouse, and sell them to the local butchers. I thought, *I could get involved here.*

Dad didn't help with the pigs. He was still smart, with his man bag on. His dementia had trapped him in the Nineties. Instead, he would sing lovely songs. My favourite was, 'If my friends could see me now'.

There were rats everywhere. Dad wasn't frightened of rats, but I was. When one rat came up, he went, 'You're frightened, aren't you?' He loved that I had a weakness.

I said, 'No, I'm not frightened.' The rat ran over his foot but he did not say a word. It came near me and I went, 'Hold up!' Dad started giggling.

A lot of healing went on. I was still learning the light and the dark. I believe God cut me to the core to get rid of all my ways – all my masks – and to get to the real Michael. God cleaned house in a very, very deep way.

One of the guys on the farm, Mark, was the number-one fan of Bob Geldof's band, the Boomtown Rats. He used to be at all of their shows, so they had got to know him. When they wanted to relaunch their career, they decided to rent the house for one week every month, for six months, starting at the beginning of 2013.

Kim asked me whether I minded and I said, 'No, not at all.'

I used to love it when they came. Bob and all the guys turned up. Bob was a really nice man, very bright and well-mannered, and all the guys were really good chaps.

I got on very well with them, so this was one of the nicest times at the farm. They used to practise in this massive white room, and I would entertain and cook for them.

The band had signed a contract to play at the Isle of Wight Festival. They weren't allowed to do gigs anywhere before that. However, we got them to play at a pub round the back of Gatwick. It wasn't official – they said that they were just rehearsing – but we filled the pub, right down to the garden. I remember Bob walking on stage. Someone shouted, 'Cor, he doesn't half look like Bob Geldof.'

I said, 'It is him.'

'Oh no, shut up!' the guy said. He just couldn't believe it.

Bob was at the farm in April 2014 when his daughter Peaches died of a drug overdose. I spent a lot of time with them. They then went on tour. I travelled with them a couple of times, including backstage at the Isle of Wight Festival, which was fantastic.

My dad's dementia was getting worse and worse. During the night, he'd sometimes wake me up with a knife in his hand; not to stab me, but he was reliving his youth. He knew that I was in trouble and he wanted to go and hurt people on my behalf. I think if we'd let Dad loose, he would have done it.

As July approached, I began to feel a bit uncomfortable and angry. It happened every year around the anniversary of Martin's death. I went to see my mum in London. She said, 'That's funny. I start feeling that way too.' Mum and I could always have an open conversation. I talked about how I had said goodbye to Martin a few years ago on Clapham Common.

'You know what, Mum? You've got to let it go,' I said.

'Son, I don't want to. I'm quite happy missing my son and feeling this pain. I always knew Martin wasn't going to live longer than twenty-one years.'

There was a level of unconditional love between Martin and Mum, which she had for me too, but mine was always blemished with a problem. With Martin, the communication of love that they had for each other was pure, holy, and incredible. Dad's love wasn't. Neither was mine; there was always something.

I was still very close to my nephew Charles, Martin's son, who I loved as if he was my own. A few days later, he was driving me home and stopped the car.

He said to me, 'You want me to love Martin. I know you do. But I can't tell you that I do, because I didn't know him. I never met him, Michael. You'll never get that wish. I can't love someone I don't know.'

I thought it was quite an adult thing to say. I turned around and said to him, 'Okay, do you love yourself?'

He said, 'Well, yes.'

I said, 'No, do you like yourself?'

'Yes,' he said.

Then I said, 'Then you like your dad. Because you are my brother's son.'

I returned to the farm and started up a little prayer group. The Pentecostal preacher, Sister Kate, came down on Thursdays and a few of us would get together. We'd listen to the Word of God and pray. They all thought we were mad on the farm. But people were starting to ask me to help their kids, who were on drugs, and I was helping a lot of them.

In November 2013, Nicky Gumbel sent *GQ* magazine down to the farm. They were doing a story on Alpha in Prisons. I remember being so touched by what Nicky said about me in the article. 'God could not have chosen a better messenger. St Paul was a bright guy, which was what was needed in the Roman world, and in the prison world, Michael was the classic guy to choose.'

I saw Nicky a few weeks later when I went to drop off his Christmas tree. I managed to hit my head on the boot as I was getting the tree out of the car. It really hurt. As he was talking, the pain was killing me. He went, 'Are you okay? You'll be all right, a tough boy like you'. I wanted to stamp on his toe.

'Are you still on the farm?' Nicky asked.

'Yes,' I said. 'Me and my dad are hiding out.'

'How exciting.'

My grandchildren, Paddy, Nancy, and Gracie, used to come and spend time on the farm. Their mothers were very neat and tidy. Aimee and Beth used to pack the kids off to the farm with beautifully ironed clothes, pants, socks, T-shirts, and trousers for three days. But I never used to give them their own clothes to put on; they used to wear old jumpers of mine with Wellington boots. We had so much fun. I used to cook them breakfast, take them for walks, and feed the pigs. That year, all of my family came down for Christmas. Dad was incredible with the grandkids – he made sure that every one of them had a fiver in their Christmas card.

On Boxing Day, Kim asked me to do the pigs. What I used to do was put my clothes on quickly, go and feed the pigs, then come back, leave my clothes in the garage and have a shower. It only took 20 minutes. But I got a bit lazy. Where the pigs were kept was empty stables that had been converted into pens. I used to go round to every gate and feed them. When you feed pigs, they scream like there's no tomorrow. But there was a little walkway in between the pens, which was covered in mud and straw. That Boxing Day, to cut corners and make it quicker, I drove the farm's little golf cart along the walkway.

I had been told never to do that, but I didn't take any notice. That day there was torrential rain. Then there was all the pigswill, and rats were running everywhere. As I went to move the golf cart, I realized it was stuck in the pig manure. Though I was revving it, the cart was beginning to sink. One of the guys, who worked on the farm, was looking at me and laughing his head off. I was a novice at this.

By now, I was getting angry. I said to the guy, 'Give us a hand.' He came over and helped me.

He said, 'What you need to do is get those two planks of wood and put them under the back wheels. Then all I want you to do is push and the tractor will pull you out.'

I was in the middle of the golf cart so the spray wasn't touching me. But when the guy said, 'Push harder,' I tried and fell.

It looked like I was doing a dive into the swimming pool. I tried to prevent myself from going down, but not only did I go in with my hands, it also covered my face so I could taste it. The geezer was crying with laughter and I wanted to hit him. I was covered head to toe; it was in my eyes and all my hair. I had to walk back round to the house. Everyone found it hilarious.

By now, I was struggling with Dad. His dementia had got worse and worse. It was a real ordeal for me. On good days, he would come out into the garden. We had moorhens, deer, and a beautiful pond. He loved all that. On bad days, he would just stay in his bedroom and feed bread to the mice that used to come up to the bottom of his bed.

Sometimes Dad would stare at me. I would stand there and look back. It was very sinister, like when I was kid and he used to check up on me in the bathroom.

One morning, I went into Dad's bedroom to find him on the floor. He'd had seven strokes. It looked like coffee was everywhere, but it was blood. He had hit his head on the side. Dad was just lying there. He said, 'I'm gone.'

I phoned the ambulance. As they closed the doors, I remember looking at Dad. All he did was stare at me. He didn't give me a look of sorrow; he gave me a look from my school days, like *Oi, hold your chin up. Oi, hold yourself together.* When the ambulance left, I burst out crying.

They took him to Reigate hospital to die. But my old man wasn't having any of it. Dad was tough. We then got him into a care home, but it was a complete nuthouse. There were men and women walking about naked, screaming and shouting. We finally got Dad into a lovely care home. A Victorian house in a pristine spot in Reigate, it was a very small hospital with about forty patients. It was the sort of place where you could go for a walk and not be disturbed. There were a few horses, dogs running past, and the sound of a farmer on his tractor.

In the meantime I left the farm. Kim was a dear friend from back in the day, but there was a lot of historic stuff with our parents and, in the end, she assumed that I was there to have them over, rather than look after the house. It wasn't true, but eventually the police came, said that they'd heard I was in a lot of trouble, and asked me to leave. It just ended overnight. My dog Meg was packed off to live with Tracy and I returned to London.

21. RESTORATION

After the farm, I had nowhere to go. A mate of mine called me. We'd been at Ford Prison together and been friends forever. He had the same birthday as me. My mate said, 'I've got a flat you can live in. No rent.'

It was in a real tough hard place in Croydon, where the Somalian dealers were selling crack. They said, 'You're either police or an American tourist.'

I replied, 'No, I am from Battersea and an ex-criminal.' I then started telling them about Jesus.

Twice a week I would visit Dad in the care home. At times, I couldn't afford to get there, but Dad gave me his pension for the train fare. At first, we all felt sorry for Dad being in a care home. Then he grew in stature by the way he conducted himself. Dad was impeccable and made the best of the care home. He was proper brave, taking dementia right on the chin. It's like Dad went, *I am here now and I am going to get on with it.* He fought like Muhammad Ali in that home and I regained my respect for my dad. He had always believed in God, but there was this fear: he would stand and fight the biggest man in the world but be petrified, like I was, of strange stuff. Death frightened him. But in the end he met it as good as gold.

Once he was in the care home, our times together abounded with grace and we began to clear up the debris between us. As much as Dad had both a confrontational and a jealous spirit, there was love in that environment too. The carers loved me and my family coming to visit, because we turned it into a party. We would be singing, doing karaoke, and having fun in the garden. Instead of telling us to be quiet, they would encourage it and bring us pots of tea and sandwiches. The one thing that they couldn't get their head around was how close we all were. When we moved, we moved as a unit. My mum would visit once a week and sit there holding Dad's hand.

In the meantime, I felt called back to my first wife, Daniella. I went out to Spain and saw her. We had been estranged for 25 years but it was always a strong relationship. The question of whether we'd done the right thing splitting up was always in my heart and in hers, yet the historic pain was still there.

Daniella and I became very close. I thought, *Maybe this is meant to be.*

Her cousin said to me, 'Well, she's never stopped caring for you.'

I said, 'It's the same for me.'

She said, 'Just be gentle with her.' Daniella was going through the menopause and it was really difficult.

During the summer of 2016, Dad contracted pneumonia and was given four days to live. Me and my sister Karen rushed to his bedside, where we sat holding his hand and singing to him. But the old man kept going. Every week we would rush up, but then the doctors kept saying that he was getting better.

One day on my way back to Croydon I got a phone call. Mum had had a turn. She had been looking for my National Insurance number, which I needed urgently but couldn't find. She climbed up on a cupboard to search for the piece of paper, but fell and broke her knee. When I rushed to see her in hospital, I was told everything was okay; she was going to be all right. But while she was there they detected a problem in her kidneys. The six-year-old boy in me came out, going, 'Mum, Mum, don't leave me'. She was the backbone of our family; everyone absolutely adored her. She couldn't die.

Mum stayed in hospital for a month. The doctors were saying all kinds of different things. I said to one of them, 'Let's just get this right. Is she going to be okay?'

He replied, 'Calm down.'

I continued, 'No, listen. I'm calm. You tell me about my mum. What is it?' I was then told that the hospital could try and get her kidneys working again, but that she could be on dialysis for the rest of her life. I thought, *She won't like that.* I said, 'But she's okay?' The other doctor said it was life-threatening. But I was looking at her and she seemed pretty cool.

It was 3 August 2016. Mum was getting worse. All the family arrived at the hospital. Brothers, sisters, children . . . it was the colourful side of the family. But Mum asked us to leave, and I was confused about that. The doctor gently told me, 'Sometimes when people know they're going to die, they ask everybody to leave.'

Back home in Croydon, I stripped naked and started marching around the room, going, 'I'm not having my mum die. She's going to be all right.' I don't know why I was naked. The phone went. It was my beautiful cousin Julia, who told me, 'You need to get back here.'

When I arrived at the hospital I was told that Mum had already died once, but they had managed to resuscitate her. I walked into her room and saw this woman I utterly adored, naked, surrounded by eight doctors and nurses who were trying to pump her back to life. They hit her body with the electricity. Mum's legs flew up into the air.

One of the doctors saw me and said, 'What's he doing here?' But I didn't take any notice. All I could think was, *Mum, don't leave me.*

Mum came back round. The doctor said to me. 'We've resuscitated your mother, but if it happens again, she'll have brain damage.' My mum went again. I flew down to my knees. 'Mum, please don't go. Lord, please in the name of Jesus.' But Mum was gone.

It was surreal. Not only could I sense that she was gone, the atmosphere had changed, the energy went.

At my mother's funeral at HTB, we all turned up in red – her favourite colour. It was like a wedding. Afterwards, a friend of mine came up to me and said, 'Of all the parties you have put on' – and I'd put on a lot of really big parties – 'your mother's funeral was the most enjoyable one.'

I am convinced she's in heaven. Her faith was like a soft pillow she would lie on. Mum loved love, whatever hat it had on, but she believed in God 100 per cent.

I didn't tell Dad about Mum's death but he knew. A mate of mine had visited him in the care home on the day of her funeral. He gave my dad some dahlias, my mum's favourite flower. When I visited Dad the next day, I saw them on the windowsill. It upset me. The following day, I came back with Karen. When she left, Dad said to me, 'Where's Mum?'

I replied, 'She's gone home and you'll see her soon.'

'No, something's not right'. To me, it was proof that no matter what had gone on, that bond of love could never be broken.

I continued to visit him at the care home in Epsom. Dementia makes some people angry, but dementia made him soft, although not weak. He knew what was happening to him and that he wasn't going anywhere.

Dad used to sit in his room and go, 'Where's my Michael? Where's Michael?' When I arrived, he would either be relieved or try to do his frightening act. 'Where have you been?' It was like I was a kid again, but I never took any notice.

Other times, he would sulk and I would go, 'Listen, if you're going to sulk, I'm going to leave.'

He'd say, 'All right,' and then we'd get back in tune. I reckon 98 per cent of our visits were brilliant.

We'd hold hands, pray, and sing. The healing which happened in that room was unbelievable. All the therapy in the world couldn't have done what prayer did in that stinky room, with a dementia-ridden man who couldn't eat. We'd had some real bad years: being involved in a million-pound crime brings trouble; prison cells bring trouble. But God used our time together in the care home for me to fall madly in love with Dad again. I put him back on the pedestal I had him on for all those years, but in a way which was respectful.

Dad then had another stroke. The care home started feeding him through his nose, but he kept ripping the tube out. In the end, I spoke to my sister and said to the doctors, 'Don't give him any medication for his chest. Let him die. It's not fair that you keep bringing him back to life. He's six stone and in a care home.'

Sometimes, my dad's great friend Beluga would visit. He was an incredible man who had supported us both through our prison sentences. We would go across to the Red Lion pub. He'd lift my dad out of the chair, then the three of us would sit at a table and reminisce about the old times. Dad and Beluga would have a beer. I can remember Beluga laughing one day at how flirtatious my dad still was with the bar staff.

Once me and Dad drove to Brighton and he had a moment of clarity. With such severe dementia, Dad felt very locked away in that car, helpless, but his inner being still showed strength and he wanted to be my dad. I was driving down the road talking about a girl. I didn't even think he was listening, he was staring out of the window. Then he did his famous thing, tapping my hand on the gear stick. He said, 'If you're trying to impress me or your friend in the car, when you speak about women, speak about them with respect.' I thought, *God, where did that come from?*

When we arrived in Brighton, we went to The Regency fish-and-chip restaurant he used to take us to when we were kids. The old place hadn't changed at all. We carried him into the restaurant and sat him in a chair, though it was a struggle for him and he wanted us to leave after a few moments. But he still had his appetite and managed to order his fish and chips. He started eating my food, calamari, and it got caught in his throat. We had forgotten that he needed his food mashed up. He was coughing and spluttering. I panicked, but Dad had the clarity and the strength to say, 'Michael, it's okay. I'm only coughing.'

That Brighton seafront held many memories for us. It was the last time he went there, so it was a fitting end. As much as it was sad, I know Dad thoroughly enjoyed himself. Subconsciously, all those moments of loving and caring for him were something that I needed. It was also something that he needed, throughout our trial and tribulation. God used that love to start putting us back together again.

At the beginning of 2017, I went on a quick trip to in Spain. I didn't have the money to go, so Beth and Perry paid for my flight. They were moving out there and wanted my help setting things up with their business, so I introduced them to a solicitor. By now, Dad had been in a care home for eighteen months. He was 85 years old and still had pneumonia, so it was a biggie for me to be going to Spain, but the doctor said, 'Come on, he's lasted like you can't believe. You'll be alright for a week'. So, on Friday, 6 January, I flew out to Marbella and a friend lent me an apartment in Fuengirola. Beth was back in London but I met up with Perry.

Only the day after I arrived, my stepsister Alice called me. 'Dad's taken a turn. All he keeps saying is, "Where's Michael?"'

But Dad had done that a number of times so I said, 'Let's see how the day goes.'

On Sunday morning, I got another phone call, telling me that Dad was bang in trouble. I spoke to the care home staff, who said, 'Look, sorry, Michael, we got things wrong. Brian's taken a turn for the worse. He's only got three days to live.' I tried to get a flight home that day but they were expensive so I booked a flight for Monday.

On Monday morning, I woke up to a phone call saying that my dad only had two hours left. I couldn't believe it. I was so upset. I rang Tracy, who happened to be half an hour from Dad's care home, and she rushed to his bedside. I then rang Beth and quietly asked her to go down there. She used to suffer with a little bit of fear, but then she would click into it and, like me, climb a mountain.

Perry came to meet me. Together, we drove to try and get a better phone signal. Amazingly I managed to get through to the mobile of one of Dad's carers and Perry pulled up on the hard shoulder. The carer put me on speakerphone so Dad heard me. He shaped up: his boy was in the room. He was responding and put his tongue out of his mouth.

The owner of the care home shouted, 'Michael, pray.'

Dad was ready to die; he was just waiting for his son's voice. I spoke to him, and I said everything that I needed to say in 4 minutes, 48 seconds. We had a million resentments to clear up, a million things to say, but nothing was said other than pure, pure love. In those few moments, the relationship between me and my dad was healed. I told him that my mother had died. He didn't like that, but I said, 'You're going to be with her in a minute.' I told him, 'Dad, don't be frightened,' and I asked the Holy Spirit to come and take him.

Just as I finished saying that, Dad died. I let out a scream: 'It's over.'

I was convinced that he had gone home. I know that he died in the presence of God. The care-home owner, who saw death every day, said, 'Michael, we've never witnessed anything like it. God was in this room.'

So I felt happy that he had died. Dad's death was a beautiful ending for me and him. For so long, Dad had been my rival and he'd created that rivalry. I didn't. But I'd played along. At the end, it was me and him, with nothing, absolutely nothing – but everything. He died with no guilt or shame, and there could've been a lot. He was an incredible human being but a broken man. I wish he'd had the knowledge of God that I have today, because deep down he was a good man. But I felt some of the badness in me relinquished when he died, as if Dad had said, 'Son, I'll take that with me. It's gone on the cross. You get on now.'

I cancelled my flight home, left my dad in the morgue at Reigate, and sat in Spain for a week. I felt a rollercoaster of emotions. I identified death with Martin dying, and that was overwhelming. But Dad's death didn't have that type of emotion; it had a romantic end-of-story feeling which made me very happy. Dad and I had been at each other for years and years – in very volatile ways. We could never communicate in a way that was acceptable for father and son. It went back to that inherited spirit of dysfunction, violence, and insanity. Yet one phone call had taken care of it all.

Dad's funeral was meant to happen in Epsom, but on my return to the UK, I moved it to Chelsea, so it could be at HTB, the same place as my mum's. I wanted my dad to wear new clothes so I went to Marks & Spencer in Battersea and picked out a lumberjack shirt, a nice pair of yellow Sta-Prest trousers, and a lovely pair of socks.

As I walked up to the counter to pay, the lady at the till said, 'What's the matter?'

I replied, 'I feel like I want to cry. My dad's died and I don't think he'll like these trousers.' I could just feel it in my spirit; it was overwhelming. The lady was very kind and I swapped the trousers.

The next day I went to see my dad's body. No one else wanted to because of the state Dad had been in before he died, but I had to go. Lillie met me in the chapel of rest. I felt nervous, frightened; childhood fear popped up. But I walked in and, I kid you not, Dad was smiling. He looked like he'd just come off the beach in Marbella. I said to him, 'You saucy b–.' There was this eerie feeling. I was nervous to touch him; I thought he would go, 'Oi!' and grab my arm. But Dad was gone. It was just his body there now, and I actually went cold because I knew I was looking at something which didn't exist no more. Lillie cried but I couldn't.

My dad's funeral was perfect. I was one of the pallbearers and in a very good frame of mind, with my wits about me. There were no disturbances in my head.

We walked into the church to the sound of a brilliant song from the Robert de Niro film, *Once Upon a Time in America*. At the front, there was a big screen showing photographs of my mum and dad. There was a great turnout. The place was full. I felt so proud as I looked around and saw how many people were there for him; people who we hadn't seen for years and years. I didn't sit in one place during the funeral, but walked around instead and sat with all these faces from way back.

I remember five real, old gangsters attended the service. I cried and they cried. And they were real gangsters who were built like that: robbed banks, smuggled drugs, and other things. But we didn't have big cars everywhere, and people in overcoats. We did my dad's funeral with humility. We showed a video of 'You've got to pick a pocket or two' from the musical *Oliver!*

We had singers, a harp player, and a few Christian songs. I shared my faith very openly in front of all the flat noses, all the villains. I felt very moved. Dad and I were two urchins who had done all sorts of very dark shenanigans over the years. We knew what poverty was like and we knew the outrageous way of life, which successful criminal activity could bring. We knew both love and hatred. But throughout this, God never left us.

I told everyone how I had prayed for the old man before he died. There was respect. My dad was a canny old boy and I don't think there were many of those about. The gangsters behind me could have his story because my dad didn't claim notoriety. He claimed nothing. He was who he was, and to be his son was hard, but we ended well.

22. WORK IN PROGRESS

After Dad and Mum died, my prayer life became a panicked prayer life. I was praying, 'Please, please, please, Lord, help me with this debt.'

I collected Dad's ashes and took them back to my half-brother Brian's flat, where I was staying. He asked, 'What have you got in the bag?'

'The old man,' I replied, taking the pot of ashes out. Brian got really frightened.

'What?'

'Dad's in the bag.'

Later I rubbed some of the ashes on my face.

I was trying to find work but couldn't find a job. I was in such doldrums after losing all of my money. So I decided to volunteer at HTB's homeless shelter.

At first, I wasn't very good at helping out. The guys could get a bit lairy and throw a few right-handers at me, so I would usher a few of them out. I then realized that you were not allowed to do that, but still it was all right because I had done it in a way that no one had got hurt.

Shortly after Dad died, I spoke at HTB about the start of Alpha. Since my life had fallen apart, for a number of years I hadn't done any work for Alpha, nor really attended HTB. But I'd always found HTB a very safe place and the church had been really supportive when my parents died. I remember Nicky's incredible kindness and compassion.

Around April 2017, a Ugandan man with very shiny clothes came up on stage at HTB. I was very moved by the way he spoke with authority, and I listened to him. He had been a Ugandan Government minister but, when a new government had come in, he was arrested and put on death row. He had been on death row for twenty years. As soon as he said that, my ears pricked up. He didn't look like a death-row candidate to me.

The man said, 'I looked out of my cell one day and saw an Alpha for Prisons advert.' My ears pricked up again.

He continued, 'I was going to die so I went and did the Alpha in Prisons course. I gave my life to Jesus.'

Listening to this man, I felt in my spirit, *That's the fruit of everything you've been through*. It was unbelievable.

They took the man off death row. He left prison, returned to work for the Government, and is now the Minister for Prisons in Uganda.

I never expected what happened next in my personal life. It began very differently from all the other relationships I'd had with women. Working at the HTB homeless shelter in 2017, I met a Kiwi called Sara, who jumped around a bit like a kangaroo and came bounding up to me. I thought, *God, she's a looker*. She had just heard me speak about my dad and was intrigued. We started chatting away. Before I knew it, a friendship had developed between us, but a pure friendship.

As I continued to work at HTB's homeless shelter, Sara and I became good buddies. She was a full-time carer for a girl called Catti, who had Down's Syndrome. When I first met Catti, I remember being a bit offish with her. But as I got to know Sara, I watched how her tender, loving care transformed Catti's life. Catti used to amaze me: she worked in the homeless shelter, cooking, cleaning, and making tea. Being around Catti, feeling her love and compassion, I learnt to reciprocate it.

That autumn, me and Sara started seeing each other. Sara was an angel. She put up with me having no money and nowhere to live; she stuck with it. Her love was a pure love, because it was action rather than emotion. Sara was spontaneously very friendly to everybody and all sorts; she had the capacity to love even the stinkiest person – everybody and everything.

I realized the Kiwis are not like us. They're outdoor people, they're like warriors. They learn how to ride a small moped or a rambling bike, or they go out climbing. Sara was like that. She'd walk 20 miles and it wouldn't even matter to her. She'd march, going, 'Come on,' which was great for me. We'd get up at 6 a.m. and meet to go for a bike ride or a long walk – real simple things. She would say, 'No, stop. We're not going to the restaurant. We've got sandwiches.'

In 2018, we went to Bologna. Before all of my troubles, I was used to the best hotels in the world. From the outside, our hotel in Bologna looked like a prison. But the room was beautiful and Sara said, 'Look, we're okay. What are you worried about? Stay here.' And it was lovely.

We visited this big Catholic church. It was an

hour-and-a-half walk, with the most beautiful view at the top. When I got to the top, Sara said, 'Did you enjoy that?'

I said, 'It was fantastic.'

The next day, we went to Venice by train. She took the breakfast from our room and turned it into our packed lunch. I loved the simplicity of it all. Sara was also not into designer labels; she could be happy rummaging around in second-hand shops looking for hidden treasures. I used to think, *my god*, and when she began to buy me stuff there, at first I told her not to. But I started to like it.

My daughter Ruby and I continued to get closer, but then trouble from my past came between us and for a number of years, the two of us didn't speak. We have now begun to communicate and Ruby recently met up with her three sisters.

That Christmas, I remember crying my eyes out to the carol of 'Silent Night'. It was so healing.

> *Silent night, holy night!*
> *All is calm, all is bright.*
> *Round yon Virgin,*
> *Mother and Child.*
> *Holy infant so tender and mild,*
> *Sleep in heavenly peace,*
> *Sleep in heavenly peace.*

Those words 'calm' and 'bright' used to really touch me. I could really sense that Christ was born. I would weep about the awesomeness of that unconditional love – it was hope. 'Silent Night' was a song I used to sing with the kids and share a good hearty tear, just one of those songs which connected me to God. My Christmases were always so special.

In the new year of 2019, I moved into a flat opposite Emmy Wilson. It was very cheap, but I struggled to pay the rent. I really struggled there, but it was the first time that Sara and I had anywhere we could be on our own.

We had had a very rocky twelve months. In September 2019, I gave up my flat and we went to see her parents in New Zealand. But when we arrived, I was stopped at Immigration because of my criminal record. I wasn't fazed, as I was used to this kind of thing, but it was a challenge.

I thought I could probably outfox Immigration but decided that I would have to lie to do it, and I didn't want that. They allowed me to stay in the country for a few days. It was pouring with rain. I went to meet Sara's mum and dad, thinking this would be difficult after what had happened, but her parents showed a lot of love and understanding. They tuned into me like there was no tomorrow.

After seventy-four hours, I had to return to the UK. I arrived back to find that my dog Meg, who I'd had at the farm, was dying. So I took a train from Heathrow to Clapham Junction, onwards to Southampton, then a boat across to the Isle of Wight, where Tracy lived. I took Meg to the vet, who said that my dog needed a £3,000 operation, but it wouldn't necessarily work.

I said, 'Let her go to sleep', and the vet agreed that was the best thing. As they put her down, I stared at Meg's face, then put my mouth towards her and she kissed me. I held her as she went. There was such a connection with me, Dad, and Meg. Her death broke my heart.

When I returned to London, I had nowhere to go. Then I got a phone call from a relative who offered me their flat, just opposite my old one in Earl's Court, so I moved in. My grandchildren would come and stay. Sara, who had also come back from New Zealand, would go round to the shop and get a colouring book and a few crayons, and we would sit with the grandkids for hours. I didn't have the funds to spoil them, so I had to do the things that grandparents do, like push them on the swings, buy an ice cream, or go out for a walk. I learnt love in action – and I really enjoyed it. Sometimes I would take them out. Paddy and I went to two FA cup finals. Nancy and I went out for a dinner date, to see *The Lion King* together, and she drove me nuts as she knew every line.

By the end of 2019, there were four more grandchildren. With Paddy, Nancy, and Gracie who had come along already, they made a grand total of seven.

My eldest daughter, Aimee, had Teddy on 2 January 2015, and Alfie on 23 February 2017. On 13 March 2019, my third daughter Beth gave birth to Noland, when she had pneumonia; he was born about four months premature. It was touch and go, but they both pulled through. I could see my dad in Noland. On 21 December 2019, Lillie gave birth to Freddy. As I had with all my other grandchildren, I fell in love with him immediately.

Whatever trouble I was in during their young lives, I loved my children and grandchildren unconditionally. At times everything in my life seemed bad, but then I would be gifted these beings, my grandchildren, and it couldn't be anything other than pure love. Every time one of them was born, it took me up a notch. Each notch was a piece of victory and love, realigning me back with reality. It felt like something had healed in my self-worth.

My grandchildren were the first people in my life that I learnt to love naturally without forcing it. It was not disturbed by any ego, pride, finances, or sexuality. It was not governed by looks, or how smart they were, or what they wore, nor by how well they could play football. It was governed by love, a very pure love. God was showing me unconditional love because I couldn't do that with my kids.

At Christmas 2019, Sara went to New Zealand again. I stayed in London. One Sunday, I was at HTB and remembered a talk given a while ago by Sandy Millar, the former vicar of HTB, who was now a bishop, about ancestral sin. The penny dropped. I thought, *That's me.* But the good news, he said, is that the future generations will be blessed.

That's my quest, I thought, *that the future generations will be blessed.*

EPILOGUE

From November 1994 to the present day, the spiritual game that I've been involved in – to fight the demons of my past – has been incredible. Sometimes I want to walk away and say, 'Drop me out', but I'm always reminded in my spirit of the truth of God. Not by radical preaching, not by peaceful preaching, but in my heart. There's something that resides in me that knows that God is real.

I want to live in my connection with God because everything's in there and I don't need anything else. Love comes from that connection, as do peace, joy, finances, friendships, and church. God said, 'Let there be light.' There was light. God speaks and stuff happens. He fights our battles, but we have to allow him to. I thank God that He helped me fight my battles. He knew what I was doing and I never got away with any of it, but He still kept loving me and blessing me.

Sara is an incredible woman with such compassion for the broken. We have a great friendship that has started to turn into something that could be our future. I know I'm hard work. Sara has been very patient and puts up with a lot, but sees the diamond in me that God's put there. What I find attractive about her is not how pretty her lips are or sexy her body is, but how wonderful her heart is. My children say she may be the only woman who I've ever listened to. They love it that she's hard on me – well, not hard, but not easy. She has taught me how to love again.

Through Sara, my life continues to be enriched by Catti. She helps me by just being herself. By the way she lives her life, Catti's enabled me to understand what love is. She has an overwhelming capacity to love people and it's not because of the particular situation; it's her heart. The amount of ability she has in her disability is incredible, and I have the utmost respect for her. From being 50 per cent disabled, she's now 80 per cent new. It's wonderful. I feel encouraged that if she can heal, anyone can.

So Sara, Catti, and I are three buddies. We all hang out and serve in the HTB homeless shelter twice a week. In between, I work at a fruit and veg stall in Earl's Court and help out with Alpha in Prisons. After many years of head-scratching, soul-searching, and tapping into the love of Jesus so they could love their neighbour, HTB must have found me very hard work. But Nicky Gumbel has always stuck by me. He's the business.

When I used to share for HTB, it had always been for different reasons. When I first came out of prison, it was my brokenness, then my shame, followed by my importance, then finally my popularity. But over the past six years, I've shared really well. I've always shared well because I've got the dialogue, but the heart was never in tune with the soul and the words – it was maybe more the head that was in control. I was taught to lie: that's what criminals do. Now, I am just very real about the darkness.

I think it is amazing, the simplicity of what love is and

yet the incredible magnitude of what love is. God's love is just love; it's not complicated. We think to surrender is weak; we think simple is stupid. But in the eyes of God, or in the Word of God, surrender is beautiful, simple is awesome, and simple is massive. The magnitude of power that unconditional love has via God is breathtaking. It's not how smart you are, it's not how sexy you are, it's not how much money you've got. Love is an action.

My grandchildren are the most amazing beautiful children I have ever met in my life. They're all my favourites, just different types. I absolutely adore every single one of them. On a scale of one to ten, the love is at ten, 24/7. I would do anything for them. When my grandchildren run into room, they go, 'Papi' and jump into my arms. They all get on with me. I'm not easy on them. In fact, I'll give it to them. But not one of my children or their partners, when I speak to their kids a little bit abruptly, will say anything.

'Behave yourself,' I say.

My grandchildren go, 'All right, Papi.' But they listen.

God has allowed me to love them unconditionally and he has allowed my heart to wake up so I can love others.

My grandchildren have made me more loving toward my girls again. There have been times when our relationships have been very fragile. Not their fault; mine. When I had everything, I thought I had a right to do exactly what I wanted to do. Deep down I knew what I was doing was wrong, but I didn't have the understanding of how to stop it. The difference with the way my children were brought up was that I used to buy their love and their friendship. The love was in my heart, but I couldn't connect with it.

My struggles have held my children back because they were frightened for Daddy, frightened for Mummy, so they never really reached their full potential. But they are now on their way.

Aimee is an incredible mother. She has a partner called David, who has been so understanding. Nancy, her eldest, is a beautiful girl, super-intelligent and very kind. The dinner dates I had with her will always be treasured memories. She has been blessed with the gift of love and the gift of being a chatterbox. I can see a wonderful life for her. Then you've got Teddy, who used to be very naughty, but he went to school and has come out a lovely boy. Teddy has a very special way about him. I find him very humbling. He has brought so much joy to us and I am looking forward to seeing him become a very strong, kind man. Alfie, the youngest one, is a dreamboat with a face to die for. He's like an all-American star with box-blond hair and big blue eyes. If looks were money, he'd be extremely wealthy. The times we spent cuddling, with me kissing his ears, were moments that healed me while I was going through so much turmoil.

My middle daughter Lillie suffered and has been a challenge. She didn't cope too well with what went on and so ran for cover. Very headstrong, Lillie was always very loyal and incredible, and stood by me. She now has a partner, Joe. My grandson Freddie has brought out the true potential in his mummy. Freddie is the peaceful one. He's so adorable, happy, handsome, and a pure soul. The smile he gave us from the beginning enriched all of us to love him in an incredible way.

Beth and Perry live in Spain. Beth's a cracker: feisty,

with a backbone. She's tested my patience, starting very young. If you ask her to do anything, even some of the big things, first of all, she says no, but then she does it. Her eldest, Paddy, was my firstborn grandchild and, as soon as I looked at him, my hardened heart began to break. I feel so honoured to call him my grandson. He has shown me so much love and given me so much hope. His sister Gracie is a knockout. I can see her as a singer-actress in a massive production. She has a natural talent, but is very humble with it. In so many ways, Gracie has brought so much fun which I will cherish in my heart forever. Noland, a miracle child, is a bruiser. I loved Noland so much the moment I saw him. The other day, I was out in the garden dancing with Gracie. Beth said, 'You've been out there for an hour and a half, Dad.'

I just said to Beth, 'My grandchildren are my healing, my life, and my vision.'

It is a pleasure to call Aimee, Lillie, and Beth my daughters. I think those years of being apart from them, the foundations of their life which Tracy built, have proved beneficial for them today, because they are three amazing mothers. I have unconditional love for them all and look forward to enjoying my family in the autumn of my life.

Tracy and I are great, great, great buddies. With all our pain, the relationship never started well, but she wanted me to be happy. I wanted her to be happy. It's been a relationship with a lot of highs, a lot of lows, a lot of fun, and a lot of sadness. She is a beautiful soul. I adore her today and would do anything for her, but I'm not in love with her. She was a victim of the insanity of Michael, and I thank God that we have a special love for each other now.

Aimee, Lillie, and Beth are in touch with Ruby. I hope that I can help Ruby when she's ready. I never wanted to reject her or disown her. I never wanted that; it was the circumstances of not being financially equipped. I hope I can be a friend to her, someone who she respects and loves. It takes time to get to know me and time to get to know her. I pray for Ruby every day and look forward to the day that God opens my heart and Ruby's so that we can meet on the level of daughter and daddy.

I'm not ashamed of my story. It's the truth. My responsibility today is to take the lies and defeat the dark. Bear Grylls, the survival writer and TV presenter, said the last 200 metres of Everest were the hardest. I feel I've been at the last 200 metres for a while now, but the Word of God says that He can heal brokenness. Do I believe in that? Yes, I do, because I bore witness in my own character. For me to stop going back to crime, and women, and all that, I felt that I was holding on to the back of an aeroplane flying across the sky. But I never stopped holding on. The process is not complete, but the mind has changed, the eyes have changed.

There's no get-out-of-jail-free card. There's no direction. There's love, there's guidance, there's prayer, but the truth can only be found in God. There's no other truth. I don't care; I've looked everywhere. There's good feelings in lots of things, from the lust in the world, such as sex or greed, to things like arguing and destruction, but none of these feelings work.

Dad's life could have been so, so different but I intend to honour that. I know that my dad – now improved and clothed in the blessing of God – is rooting for me. He's on the touchline saying, 'Go on, son', because he wants me at peace. I intend to finish well for the both of us. I don't always get it right, but I don't get it badly wrong like I used to.

When I met Jesus, I knew he was real. It's the truth. That hasn't stopped other areas of my life playing out, but God takes his time. In that time, he's taken away the sex stuff, the drugs stuff, the crime stuff, the love of money, and just stuff that used to affect me subtly, in my being.

I don't feel old. It's weird; God is restoring me to my youth. I was more tired thirty years ago. I bear witness to being set free, and I'm still working on it. It's not 100 per cent, but it's not like it used to be. The glam's gone, all my cars and businesses are gone; there were times after that when I didn't even have a tenner. But God says, 'I will restore to you all the years the locusts have eaten.' I find myself reinvented with peace. I have been in 12-step recovery for twenty-one years and, in many ways, it saved my life. Believing in Jesus takes recovery to another level, but true freedom is when we really get into who God wants us to be.

Aimee, Lillie, Beth, and Tracy are now all settling. When they're settled, it will be my turn. I want to be the last man standing and usher this through with prayer, then turn up humbly, in peace, in love, settled. I feel there's a bow and arrow pulling back my three girls and Tracy, waiting to be released to hit the bull's eye. When I am settled, when that bow is fired, I don't think the celebration is going to be 'Let's have a party.' I think it'll be, 'Dad, can we just be on our own with you for a while, and Mummy?' And we'll go somewhere, the five of us, without the grandchildren, without our partners, and just be together.

I'm not mad any more, but I'm not looking for a pat on the back. I'm looking to take life one day at a time, learning from the past, but living in the present, and hopefully bringing hope to others for the future.

I've learnt that the past gives me an opportunity to learn, to learn to respond to my experiences differently than I used to, to know that I can aim to make progress every day, and accept that this won't be perfect, and to ask God for guidance in all this, and connect to something that is bigger than me and my ego.

I think part of this is sharing my story, my experiences, to support others, to continue to serve in the prisons and elsewhere, to encourage those that are struggling: that despite all the darkness there is light beyond it, that freedom can be found from all the destruction.

I hope that people who have had similar experiences, maybe in the world of crime and violence, through abuse and trauma, people with addiction issues or debt, or who are struggling to forgive someone, or feeling empty or overwhelmed, that all these people might find a little bit of hope from this. I don't know what comes after, only God does. I don't want to be perfect, holier than thou, but I'd like to live where God wants me to live, wind up happy, and part from this world with people saying, 'You know what? He finished well.' The only way anyone can do this is to appreciate what the truth is. If we believe in that truth, then the Word of God says that the truth sets us free.

ACKNOWLEDGEMENTS

The memories from my childhood to present day are full of fun, laughter, tears, and distress. I feel honoured to have had my mother, Jean, stand by my side to the day she went home. I also feel honoured to be able to explain the gifts and the curse that my dear dad Brian gave to me.

I would like to thank my sister Karen for always being there. You made our family proud. I am sorry if my actions spilled over into your life, but you showed true courage, love, and wisdom in dealing with it.

My darling brother Martin, you're sorely missed. We think of you most days. Thank you for having the wisdom beyond your years to stand by me through thick and thin.

To Tracy, Aimee, Lil, and Bethie, I totally adore and respect you.

To my wonderful, blessed grandchildren: Paddy, Nancy, Gracie, Teddy, Alfie, Noland, and Freddie. You are the prize amongst all prizes.

There are so many people to thank and acknowledge but I would especially like to mention:

Little Ruby.

My sons-in-law: Perry, David, and Joe.

My beautiful Helen and Charles; Charles's wife Charley; Maggie Jean, and Milo. I love you all.

My nieces and nephews: Georgia, Maddy, Samuel and Gabe, Jasper, and Jude, Louis, and Tariq. I love you guys.

My brother-in-law Mike.

Steve Doublet, Tony Assett, and Dave Bell. Rest in peace. I truly miss you.

Harry and Billy. Two wonderful men. Rest in Peace.

Ian Steers and Vicki; the Liz, Robert, John, and Clifford; Keith and John; Chilly Chris; Mark D; Tom. Thank you for being there.

Kim, Ashley, Dolcy, the Martins, and the Smiths. Love you all.

Russell Bridges. I pray things get put right. I miss you, son.

Ian and John, the camaraderie that we shared will always remain in my heart.

John Tyre. Your help will never be forgotten, thank you.

Spencer. Thank you for your help in supporting me in the dark days.

Millie. Thanks for all the laughs, special lady.

JC, Bobby McKew, Arthur Suttie, Teddy Dennis and Joe Pyle. You were true friends to my father. Thank you.

Gerry and Xanda, who I love and respect. Thank you.

Kevin H. One day we will know the truth and the truth will set us free.

Dusty. Like you said, I interfered with something that wasn't mine. You are one of my biggest regrets.

Adam and Francis. Years of fun, excitement, and disasters will remain with me. They are memories that formed us and sadly, some that broke us. Bless you two.

Nicky and Pippa; Emmy; Mark Elsdon-Dew; Paul and Amanda; Jamie; Nick; Rob; Hong; Charlotte and Caroline. Thank you for the love and patience you showed this sinner.

I want to send my love to my uncles Peter and Tom, and my aunts Veronica, Jackie, and Carol, and your families. I truly am sorry. 'Sorry' is a chuck-away word; it's by my actions that I will redeem the love and trust with you all.

My other siblings, though our relationships have been pretty dysfunctional, you're in my prayers daily.

Hattie, thank you for composing a lovely book, and Simon for his hard work.

Rose, Bengono, and all the team at HarperInspire.

Finally. To the brothers who brought me to my knees – you know who you are. The Bible says not to judge for I will be judged. I've laid bare my soul and not tried to justify my behaviour. You know what you've done. As much as it's hurt, it helped change my life.